Praise for *Reliability Engineering in the Cloud*

"As someone deeply invested in achieving operational excellence in the cloud, I found this book to be an absolute game-changer. It's a treasure trove of insights for engineering leaders and software teams eager to boost the reliability of their cloud-based systems. The authors write in a clear, engaging style that makes complex concepts easy to grasp. I was particularly impressed by how they illustrate the role of AI in helping organizations anticipate failures, automate responses, and enhance performance. In today's rapidly evolving digital landscape, I genuinely believe this resource is essential for anyone looking to stay ahead of the curve."

—Valeria Sadovykh, Technology Strategist, Microsoft

"*Reliability Engineering in the Cloud* is a must-read for anyone aiming to build resilient, scalable, and high-performing cloud systems. With actionable insights, real-world case studies, and strategies leveraging cutting-edge technologies, this book offers a comprehensive guide to ensuring system reliability, optimizing operations and fostering a culture of continuous improvement."

—Abhishek Agarwal, author of *Product Mastery*

"Dr. Breyter delivers yet another brilliant work, showcasing her position as a thought leader in enterprise transformation and technical product strategy. Her extensive hands-on experience across diverse industries, mastery of agile methodologies, and commitment to exploring cutting-edge technologies all shine through in this practical book. A must-read for any professional focused on improving service reliability and business results."

—Moshe Rasis, management consultant, executive coach, and faculty at New York University

"This is an essential guide for building resilient, scalable, and fault-tolerant systems. Covering everything from architecture design and incident response to leveraging Gen AI and OKRs, it provides actionable strategies for modern cloud environments. With a focus on automation, observability, and continuous improvement, this book equips teams to master cloud reliability engineering. A must-read for anyone aiming to deliver reliable, high-performing cloud solutions."

—Naveen Ks, Agile coach

"Whether you're a tech leader or a new engineer, this book provides practical guidance on designing resilient architectures and effective incident response using AI, ML, and gen AI to align with OKRs. Mariya Breyter and Carlos Rojas offer an indispensable resource for achieving operational excellence in the AI-cloud era."

—Piyush Sheth, senior lead (Product Enablement, Delivery) at Wells Fargo
Helping Enterprises in their Customer-Centric Product Standup, Enabling
Innovation, Delivery Journey

"*Reliability Engineering in the Cloud* by Mariya Breyter and Carlos Rojas masterfully integrates AI-driven analytics and Lean methodologies into cloud reliability engineering. This guide bridges theoretical concepts with practical applications, making it essential for those looking to optimize cloud environments. It's an indispensable resource for leaders and engineers aiming to enhance operational excellence and innovation within their organizations. A must-read for mastering cloud reliability."

—Srinivasaraju Vysyaraju, senior cybersecurity manager

"*Reliability Engineering in the Cloud* is an indispensable guide for technology leaders managing large-scale, distributed cloud systems. Breyter and Rojas deliver actionable insights on AI-driven observability, fault-tolerant architectures, chaos engineering, and operational automation, providing a comprehensive framework to ensure high availability, scalability, and resilience across mission-critical cloud environments."

—Ameesh Paleja, executive vice president, Platform Technology, Capital One

"Knowing that strategies fail without proper execution, I highly recommend this book. It equips engineering leaders to establish lean cloud reliability practices. It offers practical frameworks, crucial training, and leadership development techniques that empower cross-functional teams to drive operational excellence and continuous improvement across complex AI-supported cloud environments."

—Sara Pendergast, president, Advantage by Design, LLC

"An essential guide for enterprise leaders and engineers on how to build reliable and resilient systems to ensure long-term business success in the digital era."

—Daria Kirilenko, former senior director, Information Risk Research at Gartner

"This book is a must-read for anyone building or leading cloud-based systems. Carlos Rojas, a successful technology executive, provides a comprehensive guide to Cloud Reliability Engineering, offering practical strategies, real-world examples, and cutting-edge technologies to ensure resilient, scalable, and reliable applications. A valuable resource for technology leaders!"

—JC Gutierrez, managing director, Technology and Innovation, AWS

Reliability Engineering in the Cloud

Strategies and Practices for AI-Powered Cloud-Based Systems

Mariya Breyter
Carlos Rojas

Addison-Wesley

Hoboken, New Jersey

Library of Congress Control Number: 2025931218

ISBN-13: 978-0-13-539579-0
ISBN-10: 0-13-539579-8

1 2025

To my incredible husband, Grigoriy, who for over 30 years has been my rock, my sounding board, and my greatest inspiration—thank you for always believing in me, even when I doubted myself. Max, your success as an aerospace engineer makes me proud every day, and Anthony, your pursuit of excellence as a Presidential Scholarship student gives me hope for the positive impact of your generation on our future. You both are, in your own ways, making this world a better place.

To my extraordinary colleagues over the years: Your diversity of thought has fueled innovative solutions that continuously redefine the boundaries of what's possible in engineering and technology. To all the women in engineering and the students I mentor, thank you for your courage and vision—it's an honor to learn from you and see how you challenge the status quo. The cloud may be a powerful tool, but it's your creativity and perseverance that truly reshape our world.

—Mariya Breyter

To my entire family, especially my dad, who gave me the gift of education and taught me how to be a better man every day. To my kids and wife, who created time for me to focus on this project. To those who offered me words of encouragement during my early days, who trusted me and challenged me to think differently, and who shared their wisdom to build moments that matter throughout my life. You all have been the inspiration to work hard, learn every day, and set time aside to build the next generation of technologists. You all have shown me how important it is to elevate others, how I need to hold the elevator door for the next engineer who is going to be promoted or needs to be recognized. I came to understand early on that their success isn't just their own—it's a shared success that advances us all in society.

—Carlos Rojas

Contents

Preface

Reliability Engineering in the Cloud Is a Must: Why Your Business Can't Succeed without It

We'd like to start this book with a puzzle. Take a look at these seemingly different catastrophes and their corresponding incident summaries.[1]

- **Streamline Solutions**, a promising tech start-up specializing in e-commerce solutions, experienced rapid growth that brought unforeseen challenges. A sudden surge in website traffic during a major sales event led to a critical outage, resulting in significant revenue loss and damage to the brand's reputation.
  - What happened: Critical website outage during major sales event, lasting six hours
  - Impact: Revenue loss of $100,000, damage to brand reputation resulting in a 20% decrease in customer trust
- **HealthHub Technologies**, a healthcare start-up revolutionizing patient care with telemedicine solutions, encountered operational disruptions when a cloud service outage disrupted critical communication channels between healthcare providers and patients.

---

1. These and some other use cases in this book are fictional, though based on real companies and actual incidents. When there are actual companies mentioned, it is stated in the text and is referenced in source materials.

- What happened: Cloud service outage disrupting critical communication channels for 12 hours
- Impact: A 30% decrease in patient satisfaction, leading to 15% of patients seeking alternative telemedicine providers
- **EcoSolutions**, an environmental start-up dedicated to sustainable energy solutions, encountered operational challenges when a power outage disrupted data collection from IoT sensors deployed across renewable energy installations.
  - What happened: Power outage disrupting data collection from IoT sensors for eight hours
  - Impact: A 50% decrease in energy efficiency, leading to a loss of $50,000 in revenue due to inefficient operations
- **MegaBank Corporation**, a global financial institution, faced a public relations crisis when a technical glitch caused transaction processing delays and disrupted customer access to online banking services.
  - What happened: Technical glitch causing transaction processing delays for 24 hours
  - Impact: A 40% decrease in customer satisfaction, resulting in 10% of customers switching to competitor banks
- **AeroTech Aerospace**, a leading aerospace manufacturer, faced supply chain disruptions when a supplier's data center outage halted production operations.
  - What happened: Supplier's data center outage halted production operations for two days
  - Impact: A $1 million loss in revenue due to halted production, resulting in a 30% decrease in investor confidence
- **MedTech Solutions**, a leading healthcare technology company, faced regulatory compliance challenges when a software bug caused data integrity issues and jeopardized patient safety.
  - What happened: Software bug jeopardized patient safety, affecting the data integrity of 100,000 patient records
  - Impact: Legal fees and settlements totaling $3 million, and a 15% decrease in market share due to damaged reputation
- **Edukate LLC**, an educational technology start-up, encountered performance issues when a surge in user activity overwhelmed its cloud-based learning platform during peak exam periods.

- What happened: Scalability challenges during peak exam periods, resulting in platform downtime of four hours
- Impact: A 25% decrease in user engagement, leading to a loss of $50,000 in subscription revenue

As you can see from these examples, each situation cost millions of dollars and impacted each company's reputation and customer base. If you think this is catastrophic, imagine the consequences for organizations such as hospitals or emergency response systems, where people's lives are at stake.

We are sure that you've guessed by now what all these companies have in common: They neglected to invest in the reliability and resilience of their cloud-based systems. We will refer to this as "cloud reliability engineering" (or "CRE") in this book. In each case, the company was forced to take urgent measures to resolve situations as quickly as possible and then decided to implement long-term resilient strategies and reliability measures. So, what did these companies do? Let's review their solutions one by one.

- **Streamline Solutions:** Determined to prevent future incidents, Streamline Solutions pivoted to prioritize reliability engineering. By leveraging AI-powered predictive analytics, the company optimized resource allocation, identified potential bottlenecks, and implemented proactive measures to ensure uninterrupted service during peak demand periods.
- **HealthHub Technologies:** To mitigate similar incidents in the future, HealthHub Technologies embraced a proactive approach to reliability engineering. By integrating AI-powered monitoring and incident response systems, it achieved real-time visibility into system health, preemptively identified potential issues, and orchestrated automated failover mechanisms to ensure uninterrupted service delivery and patient care.
- **EcoSolutions:** EcoSolutions adopted a proactive approach to reliability engineering, integrating AI-powered predictive maintenance solutions. By leveraging machine learning algorithms to analyze sensor data, detect anomalies, and forecast equipment failures, EcoSolutions optimized asset performance, minimized

downtime, and maximized energy efficiency across its infrastructure.

- **MegaBank Corporation:** MegaBank embarked on a comprehensive reliability engineering initiative, leveraging AI-driven analytics to optimize system performance and enhance customer experience. By harnessing machine learning algorithms to analyze transaction patterns, predict capacity requirements, and dynamically scale resources, MegaBank strengthened its cloud infrastructure's resilience, ensuring seamless banking operations and customer satisfaction.

- **AeroTech Aerospace:** AeroTech implemented a comprehensive reliability engineering strategy augmented by AI-driven supply chain analytics. By harnessing predictive modeling and machine learning algorithms to assess supplier risk, forecast demand fluctuations, and optimize inventory management, AeroTech mitigated supply chain disruptions, ensured uninterrupted production, and maintained customer satisfaction.

- **MedTech Solutions:** MedTech invested in AI-driven quality assurance and compliance solutions. By leveraging machine learning algorithms to automate code analysis, detect potential vulnerabilities, and enforce coding standards, MedTech ensured adherence to regulatory requirements, mitigated compliance risks, and upheld its commitment to patient-centric innovation.

- **Edukate LLC:** Edukate leveraged AI-driven load balancing and auto-scaling mechanisms. By dynamically allocating resources based on user demand, optimizing application performance, and automating capacity provisioning, Edukate enhanced platform reliability, supported growing user engagement, and empowered educators and students with uninterrupted access to educational resources.

It is common knowledge that the cloud is significantly more reliable than on-premises infrastructure. This may sound easy and straightforward, but in real life, it is not. Let's take a closer look at the implementation details for Edukate's AI-driven load balancing and auto-scaling mechanisms, including specific metrics and data.

- **AI-driven load balancing**
  - Edukate's AI-driven load balancer continuously monitors user traffic and application performance metrics in real time.
  - Through historical data analysis, it predicts future user demand patterns with an accuracy rate of over 90%.
  - During peak usage periods, such as final-exam weeks, the load balancer dynamically distributes incoming user requests across multiple servers, ensuring optimal resource utilization.
  - This dynamic load balancing reduces server response time by up to 50% and prevents server overload, maintaining consistent performance levels even under heavy load.
- **Auto-scaling mechanisms**
  - Edukate's auto-scaling mechanisms automatically adjust the number of server instances based on current workload and resource utilization metrics.
  - When user demand increases, the auto-scaler provisions additional server instances within seconds, scaling the infra-structure horizontally to handle the load.
  - During peak traffic hours, the auto-scaler increases server capacity by up to 300%, allowing Edukate to accommodate sudden spikes in user activity without downtime.
  - Conversely, during periods of low demand, excess server instances are automatically terminated, reducing infrastruc-ture costs by up to 40% while maintaining performance.
- **Dynamic resource allocation**
  - Edukate's AI-driven system dynamically allocates resources to different components of the application based on work-load and performance requirements.
  - Resources are provisioned and de-provisioned in real time, optimizing CPU, memory, and storage utilization.
  - During peak usage, CPU utilization is maintained below 70% to ensure responsiveness, while memory allocation is adjusted dynamically to prevent bottlenecks.
  - By optimizing resource allocation, Edukate achieves an average server utilization rate of 80%, significantly reducing infrastructure waste and costs.

- **Optimizing application performance**
  - Edukate continuously monitors application performance metrics using AI-driven monitoring tools, including response time, throughput, and error rates.
  - Through real-time analysis, performance bottlenecks are identified and addressed promptly, resulting in a 40% improvement in application response time.
  - Database optimizations, such as query caching and indexing, reduce database response time by up to 60%, enhancing overall application performance.
  - Network optimizations, including content delivery network (CDN) integration, reduce latency by 30%, resulting in faster content delivery to users worldwide.

Overall, Edukate's implementation of AI-driven load balancing and auto-scaling mechanisms has led to significant improvements in performance, scalability, and cost efficiency. By leveraging predictive analytics and automation, Edukate ensures uninterrupted access to its cloud-based learning platform for educators and students, even during periods of peak demand.

In today's digital age, where every click and keystroke carries immense significance, the impact of CRE is hard to overstate. With the majority of systems, both internal and external, now residing in the cloud, reliability has emerged as the foundation of a successful business. From catastrophic events that have compromised millions of people to crippling service outages eroding customer trust and costing companies millions of dollars in revenue—the stakes have never been higher. With the huge repercussions of engineering misses, strong resilience engineering practices play a pivotal role in the modern business landscape and can elevate a business or destroy it. With the ability to leverage AI in multiple areas of CRE, including load balancing and auto-scaling, monitoring and alerting, risk assessment, anomaly detection, and issue resolution, CRE practices can make or break any business. As we saw in the examples, companies big and small in every possible industry can't survive without a strong CRE strategy and an AI-powered implementation of this strategy.

But first, let's start with the basics. While our primary focus in this book will be on AI-powered CRE, our secondary focus will be on efficiency, which can be achieved with Lean CRE. Lean CRE encompasses an array of principles and practices, borrowing from the traditions of Toyota manufacturing and Lean Six Sigma methodologies (see Figure I.1). These proven approaches have redefined efficiency and effectiveness in manufacturing and process optimization. Now, companies big and small are innovating in the field of CRE by adding a focus on software and people investments, and for compelling reasons. Mastering these techniques is non-negotiable for modern businesses. Successful CRE practice needs to be Lean to successfully prevent colossal failures that have happened within some of the world's most prominent companies, and to enable structured and well-thought-out CRE practices and CRE culture.

Figure I.1
Six Sigma pillars
(image: Trueffelpix/
Shutterstock)

As we dive deep into the topics of system reliability and resilience, it's crucial to understand the fundamental distinction between site reliability engineering (SRE) and CRE. While SRE primarily focuses on maintaining the reliability of individual systems and services, CRE takes a more holistic approach, encompassing the entire digital infrastructure: the cloud services used for the control plane and data plane, the tooling to monitor and observe, the AI practices to predict failure, and the mechanisms to stress-test systems using chaos engineering practices, ensuring that the entire ecosystem operates harmoniously and efficiently—with operational excellence. CRE, in this context, becomes the linchpin that holds together an organization's digital success, while AI technologies provide a strong foundation for its implementation.

CRE is not just a choice but an imperative for those organizations that aim to succeed in the digital realm. This book will show engineering leaders and decision-makers how AI-powered implementation and Lean principles can revolutionize the world of CRE and why they should be at the forefront of your organization's strategy, and offer practical advice on implementing effective reliability practices, selecting the right tools and frameworks, measuring impact through meaningful metrics, and building organizational culture that ensures sustained success in a cloud-driven ecosystem.

To summarize, reliability engineering in the cloud fundamentally changes the way organizations—big and small, profit and nonprofit, in any industry and any country—operate their systems and engineering teams. Given the rapidly evolving landscape of cloud technology, the principles of reliability engineering are undergoing a profound transformation, propelled by the integration of AI. In this book, we will take you on a transformative journey from the initial steps in building and maintaining reliable and resilient infrastructure and applications for your business, to nurturing CRE culture across the company. We will discuss the best strategies to address recovery, dissect resilience challenges, implement AI-driven frameworks, and provide the foundation that will fortify your business's digital infrastructure. It is time for your company to rewrite your engineering playbook using the methodologies and best practices described in this book. Let the journey begin.

Who Is This Book For?

This book will benefit organizations responsible for building systems in the cloud, and those engineering leaders who need to set an enterprise-wide strategy with thousands of applications and dependencies. Think of it like a corporation with hundreds or thousands of dev teams. This book serves as both the framework and a reference to two groups of readers.

The first group consists of enterprise leaders, from director and VP level to heads of specific businesses, who are looking to increase the reliability and scalability of their systems in the cloud, the efficiency of their operations, and their need for faster incident response while automating their operations to improve time to restore and time to detect to the maximum possible extent. These leaders know that operational agility and chaos experimentation bring a culture of continuous improvement built on collaboration and knowledge sharing among teams.

The second group includes engineers and software teams directly involved in or responsible for cloud applications' reliability. The frameworks and guides described in the book will allow them to build effective strategies, promoting chaos engineering practices, observability and monitoring techniques, disaster recovery exercises, reliability metrics, fast data-driven decision-making, and practical examples of techniques and tooling for success. Given the lack of both literature on the topic and established frameworks, this group of readers will benefit from having practical, domain-specific approaches and examples that they can apply to their organizations and teams.

For both groups, adopting modern CRE practices will better position their organizations to build and maintain resilient systems that meet their customers' demands to achieve their business goals effectively. This book focuses on examples and techniques used with cloud providers such as AWS, GCP, and Azure.

Register your copy of *Reliability Engineering in the Cloud* on the InformIT site for convenient access to updates and/or corrections as they become available. To start the registration process, go to informit.com/register and log in or create an account. Enter the product ISBN (9780135395790) and click Submit. If you would like to be notified of exclusive offers on new editions and updates, please check the box to receive email from us.

Acknowledgments

To my colleagues at some of the world's most innovative tech and financial services companies, your insights, dedication, and collaboration have been invaluable in shaping this book. And to my customers, your challenges have fueled my customer obsession and driven me to dig deeper into what it means to be truly reliable in the cloud.

To every reader who picks up this book, my hope is that it inspires you to act boldly and make our digital world more secure and its information accessible to all. A special thank-you to my coauthor, Carlos Rojas—your leadership continued to pave the way for transformation at a leading cloud provider and now at a global financial services company. Your vision for positive change is nothing short of inspiring.

Here's to the next generation of innovators, the ones who will push the boundaries of cloud reliability even further.

—Mariya Breyter

To my peers, leaders, teams, and friends who worked with me to transform companies during my career: For the trying moments when we collectively learned something new, I am confident most of those became components shared in this book. The concepts of reliability engineering started way before we even had the cloud. Our learnings determined how today the most important companies run their critical services in the cloud.

To every reader who decides to invest in CRE, my goal is that you implement at least one bold idea from this book to make your organization more reliable. This book will open the world of ideas to continue to invest in the highest engineering standards in recent times.

A special thank-you to my coauthor, Mariya Breyter—your leadership while we worked at AWS and your friendship outside of work have no limits and inspired me to complete this amazing project. Your vision of continued improvement and dedication to be the best is simply contagious.

—Carlos Rojas

About the Authors

Mariya Breyter is a technology executive, product leader, and educator with experience ranging from leading technology companies and government jobs to versatile corporate experience in cloud services, healthcare, financial services, media, and education. She takes pride in leading high-performance organizations in building technology products that delight customers, whether it is cloud services at a leading cloud provider, the online consumer bank Marcus by Goldman Sachs, an educational start-up incubator at Kaplan Test Prep, or a simplified global claims system at UnitedHealth Group. Her book *Agile Project and Product Management*, published in 2022, was added to Amazon's list of the top 100 books on Agile and to Book Authority's list of the "Best Agile Software Development Books of All Time," and her article on Agile frameworks was selected as part of the top Agile Articles 2020. Mariya has a PhD in computational linguistics and a post-doctorate degree from Stanford University. Mariya also teaches Agile project management, IT principles, and organizational transformation courses to graduate students at New York University. Her passion is to help others achieve their professional growth. She founded Agile Practitioners Meetup in New York, organized sessions for Women in Agile/New York, and led Mentoring Circles at the Grace Hopper Celebration. Mariya's motto is, "Lead with passion, guide with purpose, inspire with innovation."

Connect with Mariya: https://www.linkedin.com/in/mariyabreyter/

Carlos Rojas is a former Amazon Web Services (AWS) engineering leader; is a technology advisor with a certification in AI from Massachusetts Institute of Technology; and has 25+ years of experience in application development, reliability engineering, operational excellence, and IT shared services, with a proven record of success within financial, telecom, government, and health IT. Carlos is well known across multiple industries for building and transforming teams. Carlos began working as a freelance software developer in 1995 when the internet was looming. Following that, for a decade he fulfilled his entrepreneurial drive with a tech start-up called Cascade Technologies. Over the past several years, Carlos used his skills to build and transform teams into forward-thinking industry leaders in multiple leadership roles. As the global head of Region Build Automation at AWS, Carlos was part of the engineering leadership team responsible for orchestrating the launch of new regions across the globe. In 2022 he came back to a major bank as the vice president of Cloud Reliability Engineering, responsible for reimagining customers' digital experiences and improving the operational excellence of their applications.

Connect with Carlos: https://www.linkedin.com/in/carojas77/.

The combined in-depth experiences in CRE, Lean, cloud services, and enterprise engineering allow the authors to view enterprise needs from multiple perspectives. Their prior experience at AWS gives them a joint perspective on successfully applying these practices at a significant scale, and their network of content providers with specific domain expertise makes this a must-have book.

Chapter 1

Reliability Engineering in the Cloud

How to Design, Build, Operate, and Stress-Test Highly Reliable Systems

Welcome, cloud enthusiasts! Let us begin by explaining the terms "cloud," "resilient," "reliability," and "engineering," and why these are a prerequisite for a successful implementation of cloud strategies for applications in your organization.

Cloud

Cloud does not really need a description, but for most concepts in this book, it is foundational and one of the key requirements to ensuring resilient and reliable systems. The cloud offers the capability to have applications dispersed across different geographies—also known as "regions" in Amazon Web Services (AWS), Microsoft Azure, and Google Cloud Platform (GCP). Regions and Availability Zones (AZs) are fundamental concepts in cloud computing, but their implementation can vary across different cloud providers. AWS's definition and approach are widely regarded as effective and advantageous due to their clear isolation, redundancy, scalability, and consistency. According to this definition, each region allows those applications to have similar designs and stacks in different AZs[1] within that same region. Each AZ is also backed by multiple data centers in different locations. With the right architecture designs, configurations, and engineering practices, you can minimize the impact of application downtime for your customers. Without the cloud infrastructure and with the lack of elasticity, it will be difficult to accomplish a higher level of resilience and reliability, because of the cost that organizations need to carry.

Resilience

Resilience is defined as the capacity for an application to withstand difficulties or recover quickly from them. Essentially, it represents how "tough" a system or component is when faced with challenges. The foundational design principles of resilient architecture involve decomposing your application and services into small, loosely coupled, stateless building blocks. These building blocks communicate with one another via application programming interfaces (APIs) and can be managed through dynamic configuration without manual intervention. Achieving massive scale necessitates a commitment to automation and tooling. As a result, your application can continue to operate even when dependencies encounter issues. Designing an application for resilience requires thoughtful consideration of isolation, retry strategies, circuit breakers, fallbacks, failovers, monitoring, and observability, among other factors.

Reliability

Reliability refers to how customers perceive the service, capabilities, dependability, and overall experience provided by the systems

---

1. In GCP, the equivalent of Availability Zones are referred to as Zones, while regions serve the same purpose as in AWS and Azure, representing distinct geographic locations with multiple data centers.

within your organization for their day-to-day activities. To ensure a reliable customer experience, your systems must exhibit traits such as resilience, fault tolerance, and high availability. While many companies can implement various specifications, deployment patterns, and configurations to achieve these goals, few can accurately measure the resilience of their systems. Often, companies gauge success based on the number of incidents they have experienced; however, this approach is reactive and only considers customer impact after the fact. A truly reliable system is proactive and seeks to identify signs of service degradation, also known as "slow burns," before customers experience serious disruptions. Figure 1.1 illustrates reliability and resilience as the primary characteristics of any system.

Resilience: The capacity to withstand or to recover quickly from difficulties; toughness.

Reliability: The quality of being trustworthy or of performing consistently well.

Figure 1.1
Roles and definitions of reliability and resilience (image: Bannafarsai_Stock/Shutterstock)

Engineering

Engineering is the art of making magic happen: If you can think it, you can achieve it with engineering excellence. In this book, you will find detailed information about some of these concepts and the strategies to achieve higher levels of reliability for your cloud-native applications. With a focus on various cloud-related topics, including architectural patterns and best practices, as well as firsthand experiences from leading cloud service providers such as AWS, GCP, Azure, and other technology companies, you'll gain insights into modern practices of building resilient applications in the cloud. From fault tolerance to automated recovery mechanisms, each chapter provides practical examples illustrating proven engineering strategies for your companies to protect your business by building and maintaining resilient and reliable systems. In addition, the book offers insights into various techniques for accurately measuring the reliability of your applications, empowering you to make informed decisions and continuously improve your engineering practices.

Engineering Excellence

In successful companies across all industries and geographies, engineering leaders invest in cloud-resilient and reliable architectures as part of their engineering excellence practices deliberately rather than by accident. These companies intentionally, consciously, and knowingly make investments in how they design, build, and operate their applications. These companies do not compromise on how to fearlessly satisfy their customers with amazing engineering solutions. These companies embed resilience and reliability engineering within their business design, product design, engineering design, execution, and operations. Even when systems fail, these companies lead with a resilient design mentality, learn from the failure, invest in making applications across the company in compliance with these insights, and remove anti-patterns as a must-do versus just another industry technique. They implement every engineering practice to succeed in the market.

While different providers embrace cloud-resilient designs in diverse ways, with different services and design approaches, all of them align on principles and patterns of the major points of reference from the industry.

Dr. Werner Vogels, CTO of Amazon.com, stated:

> "Everything fails all the time, so design and plan for failure and nothing fails."

This is a great premise to discuss why your organization needs a cloud-resilient strategy.

According to GCP, a well-designed application is capable of scaling up and down in response to changing demand, while also demonstrating resilience in the face of service disruptions. Achieving these characteristics necessitates meticulous planning and design.

Similarly, Microsoft Azure defines resilience as the system's capability to recover from failures and maintain functionality. When designing and implementing applications, it's crucial to account for the specific failure modes inherent to each technology.

For further exploration, Microsoft provides architecture diagrams, technology descriptions, real-world examples of cloud architectures, and solution ideas for common workloads within its Azure Architecture Center.

Mark Russinovich, CTO and Technical Fellow of Microsoft Azure, stated:

> "The importance of application reliability cannot be overstated in today's digital landscape. As we rely on digital technologies for communication, commerce, and various daily tasks, smooth and consistent operation of applications has become crucial. Users expect applications to be available and responsive, regardless of the platform or device they are using. In the realm of e-commerce, finance, healthcare, and other critical sectors, application reliability becomes paramount. Whether gearing up for a seasonal event like Black Friday, handling tax filings, or striving to meet performance requirements during application

development, ensuring uninterrupted service is crucial. Downtime or glitches in applications can lead to significant financial losses, damage to reputation, and user dissatisfaction. As technology continues to advance, the emphasis on application reliability will only intensify, highlighting the need for reliable apps."

A bad experience is all it takes to shake a customer experience with your organization and the products or services you provide. When your systems are down, you risk not only losing revenue, but also damaging the organization's reputation for delivering a pleasant experience—or even worse, the organization's value. With this book, you will learn the practices, tools, and techniques to create your strategy, one that aims to do the following.

- Recover from failures while minimizing customer impact.
- Drive your business objectives with engineering practices.
- Document decisions and trade-offs to run your systems.
- Identify, manage, and take intelligent risks.
- Share learnings broadly and improve your systems continuously.
- Measure customer experience and know how to act before it is compromised.
- Create a culture of innovation, engineering, and reliability across application teams.
- Know what causes a workload to fail, and introduce refinements to "learn from mistakes."
- Safely introduce intentional failure by stress-testing your apps to anticipate and prevent failures.

More importantly, this book offers strategies with practical references (how-to guides, checklists, questionnaires), use cases, and industry examples to implement across applications in your organization. Think of it as a learning mechanism to elevate your engineering posture so that you can implement resilient systems for an improved customer experience. This book is intended to promote conversations to raise the knowledge of your organization, rather than being taken as a checklist to push down to your engineering teams. To successfully implement any of these strategies, you will need participation from your Engineering and Product departments and from senior leadership.

How to Design and Build Resilient and Reliable Applications

It's easy: Simply leverage the power of cloud-native architectures, constantly measure how reliable your applications are, create a culture of engineering excellence in your company, and leverage the different services offered by cloud providers such as AWS, GCP, and Azure.

The paragraphs that follow outline some sample design strategies to get you started and thinking ahead.

Let's begin with a standard AWS cloud-native multi-AZ architecture design that represents a simplistic yet common design pattern. Figure 1.2 illustrates the deployment of application compute resources such as lambda functions, containers running in AWS ECS, and Fargate. Additionally, it showcases the capabilities for intersystem communication. In this scenario, communication can be facilitated using Amazon Simple Notification Service (SNS) queues and Amazon Simple Queue Service (SQS). Step functions offer orchestration capabilities for coordinating various steps in your solutions, while EventBridge provides a mechanism for event-driven communication.

Many cloud providers now offer purpose-built, commercially available, and hardened databases. For example, teams utilizing AWS can leverage Amazon Relational Database Service (RDS) Aurora for their relational database needs. For more robust multiregion scenarios, DynamoDB offers global table functionality. Additionally, Amazon Simple Storage Service (S3) storage can be utilized for data lakes, analytical processing, and robust machine learning (ML) use cases.

To compare and contrast, let's now explore a similar example from GCP. Through proper design, organizations can optimize costs by adjusting resource allocation based on demand, ensuring high performance without compromising user experience. This approach allows applications to maintain excellent performance even during periods of high traffic volume, such as Black Friday, seasonal

Figure 1.2
Standard multi-AZ
deployment patterns

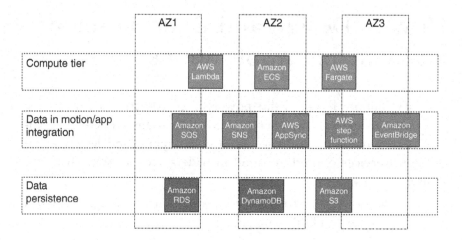

travel peaks, promotions, and tax season, while still maintaining cost-effectiveness and elasticity.

GCP provides a range of services and features to assist in building resilient applications.

- GCP services are available in regions and zones globally, allowing organizations to deploy their applications according to availability requirements.
- Compute Engine instance groups and Google Kubernetes Engine (GKE) clusters can be distributed and managed across zones within a region for improved resilience.
- Compute Engine regional persistent disks are synchronously replicated across zones within a region, ensuring data integrity and availability.
- GCP offers global load balancing capabilities, enabling traffic redirection to healthy regions nearest to users for optimal performance.
- GCP's serverless platform includes managed compute and database products with built-in redundancy and load balancing features.

How Do You Know Your Application Is Truly Resilient and Reliable?

A key element of ensuring that resilient applications are always on (24/7/365) is the ability to do the following.

- Monitor and observe your applications.
- Conduct chaos engineering experiments to stress-test their capabilities. **Chaos engineering** is the practice of intentionally introducing controlled failures into systems to identify weaknesses, improve resilience, and enhance overall system reliability (more on this in the next section).

In terms of monitoring and observability, several tools in the market offer out-of-the-box capabilities to alert on performance, correlate data to find root causes, and troubleshoot issues. Cloud monitoring provides metrics across your applications and infrastructure components, helping development and site reliability engineering (SRE) teams make data-driven decisions about the performance and health of applications. For example, tracing is a form of observability that helps engineering teams capture the end-to-end flow of a given transaction. To implement tracing, you should select a suitable tracing framework and tool such as OpenTelemetry, Jaeger, Zipkin, AWS X-Ray, or Azure Application Insights. A great applicability of AI is predictive tracing, which is used to continuously and intelligently anticipate and mitigate issues before they happen.

What if You Find Potential Issues?

You have nothing to worry about. You will find these, and when you do, chaos engineering and change management will be your best friends.

Chaos engineering is how you inject failure into a controlled environment, how you understand the behaviors of your applications, and how you document findings and remediate those potential issues before they impact your customers.

Change management gives you the ability to take those findings and make them actionable such that software development teams can remediate and test again. The ultimate goal is to avoid incidents, or to learn how to resolve them in a timely manner if they happen again. The best mechanism to test such disruptions is called "game days." These are usually led by a centralized team to plan, execute, coordinate, and report on the findings and actions taken by application teams.

Your organization needs to define and comply with the established chaos engineering and change management practices. This means setting clear expectations for remediation when an issue is identified. Executives and engineering leaders must think about operational excellence practices and commit to operational metrics and targets that will help determine the reliability of their systems.

Will Stress Testing Help Uncover All Potential Scenarios?

Not really. It is impossible to cover 100% of failure scenarios, and that is why establishing operational excellence mechanisms to review findings, share learnings, and set plans of attack is of critical importance.

Normally, we can divide failures into two different groups.

1. Those failures that we recognize, that we have experienced before, that we must prepare for, and where there is a playbook to solve for without skipping a single step (the key here is execution and documentation).
2. Those failures that we do not recognize, where we need our incident response team to work hard and fast to restore services to business as usual ASAP through detailed investigations. In this case, it is important to conduct incident analysis and remediation practices once we have understood and recognized a root cause.

Independently from which scenario incidents fall under (group 1 or 2), operational excellence in partnership with change management is there to identify learnings, change the culture of the organization, minimize waste, and continuously improve engineering practices—all to provide customers with a reliable experience and ensure limited disruption of their systems. Being aware of the new behaviors or techniques, or the areas that need to be improved, is critical to have learning opportunities after each incident.

Setting Operational Excellence metrics to ensure your applications are cloud resilient by design

Once executives and engineering leaders define operational excellence practices, they need a mechanism to ensure that these practices are well-defined and followed by the application teams. In other words, they need to know what success looks like. Is the organization on the forefront of engineering excellence, or is it lacking in specific areas?

This book will introduce you to how reliability metrics and objectives and key results (OKRs) apply to resilience engineering, and how anyone within the organization can take ownership of measuring and improving the quality and outcomes of their applications. Objectives help set up clear outcomes for the business and engineering operations while key results offer clear measures for each of these outcomes and timelines. Reliability metrics such as median time to detect, time to restore, and incidents per volume of changes also help drive the culture of operational excellence while guiding teams to successfully report on the outcomes of resilient designs.

These measurements cannot be done manually. Tooling is an important aspect of automating the actions from the learnings and metrics. In this case, it is important to have capabilities to observe and monitor applications at a level of detail that will pinpoint exactly what the problem is without losing time to detect, or time to engage, or time to restore an incident. When there are thousands of applications, services, endpoints, regions, AZs, databases, and dependencies, it is difficult and expensive to scale by adding humans to the operation. Therefore, tooling is the first approach to consider when teams are expected to automate every action.

Figure 1.3 illustrates a sample dashboard that allows organizations to observe system health in real time.

Figure 1.3
Sample dashboard (image: Andrey_ Popov/Shutterstock)

Leveraging Lean Principles

Lean core principles, rooted in Lean manufacturing practices developed by the Toyota Production System in the mid-20th century, focus on maximizing value while minimizing waste. The goal is to create more efficient processes by identifying and removing activities that do not add value. This approach stems from Toyota's strategies for achieving just-in-time manufacturing and quality improvement, which have become the foundation for Lean practices applied across various industries, including technology and cloud engineering.

Continuous improvement, or "Kaizen," is a key aspect of Lean philosophy. It involves constantly analyzing processes to identify and implement incremental changes that improve efficiency, reliability, and performance. In cloud resiliency engineering, continuous improvement emphasizes monitoring systems and iterating on designs to ensure high availability and disaster recovery while incorporating feedback loops for ongoing enhancement. This aligns with Lean's emphasis on problem-solving and developing a culture that encourages collaboration and accountability among all team members.

Waste elimination, known as "Muda" in Lean terminology, is equally critical. Waste can manifest in cloud operations as excess resource consumption, inefficient processes, or underutilized assets. Lean encourages engineers to optimize cloud environments by automating processes, streamlining workflows, and employing data-driven strategies to reduce redundancy and resource wastage. By applying Lean principles to cloud resiliency engineering, teams can achieve cost savings, improved system performance, and a more sustainable approach to managing infrastructure.

Leveraging Artificial Intelligence

A strategy to consider for ensuring system health is leveraging AI and large language models (LLMs). These technologies can enhance reliability engineering by providing real-time insights into system performance, identifying potential failures before they escalate, and streamlining incident management. AI-powered monitoring tools can analyze vast amounts of telemetry data, detect anomalies, and proactively suggest mitigation strategies. By integrating LLMs into incident response workflows, organizations can reduce downtime, improve root cause analysis, and ensure that teams are better prepared to handle recurring issues.

When teams experience incidents, they can interact with LLM-based systems in plain natural language to quickly retrieve the most recent status of an incident. Instead of sifting through multiple dashboards, logs, or tickets, engineers can simply ask AI-powered assistants for a real-time summary of affected components, impacted services, and ongoing remediation efforts. Additionally, AI can prioritize alerts based on severity, historical patterns, and business impact, allowing teams to focus on critical incidents rather than being overwhelmed by excessive noise.

Beyond real-time status updates, LLMs can also automate the creation of essential documentation, such as incident summaries, post-incident reports, and corrective action plans. AI-driven tools can extract key insights from system logs, team discussions, and historical incident data to generate detailed memos that help teams understand what happened and how to prevent similar issues in the future. This automation reduces the administrative burden on engineers, enhances knowledge sharing across teams, and ensures a consistent approach to incident management and resolution."

Leveraging Value Stream Mapping

VSM is a Lean management tool used to visually represent the steps and activities involved in delivering a product or service from start to finish. It provides a detailed overview of the entire process, including the flow of materials, information, and actions, to identify areas of waste, inefficiencies, and opportunities for improvement. VSM helps organizations streamline processes, optimize workflows, and enhance overall efficiency by identifying bottlenecks, redundancies, and areas for improvement within the value stream. This technique is extremely helpful when defining your standard operating procedures (SOPs) and specifying ownership by role.

It is important to look holistically across multiple related processes and areas of impact—this is where Lean practices come into play. In Lean, there is an important concept of a **value stream**, an approach aimed at optimizing processes and eliminating waste to create more value for customers, including all the actions, information flows, and resources involved in the process. It starts with value stream mapping (VSM) to identify the steps and activities involved in the design, build, and operation stages—from the initial development of a system or feature to its deployment, monitoring, incident response, and ongoing maintenance, identifying waste and suggesting opportunities to streamline and optimize.

Culture and Values

We have been discussing systems and processes, but this requires a solid foundation in the company's culture and values. Engineering leaders need to start by building a psychologically safe environment and culture of innovation throughout the organization. Operational excellence includes a culture of leadership and ownership, being vocally self-critical, welcoming failure and learning from it, collaboration, and fast decision-making. Mistakes are expected, and learning from them is a big part of growth. The impact of failure is huge and potentially damaging to a company's reputation, and leaders need to build a culture of learning from failures and pivoting for excellence.

Operational Excellence

Engineering leaders need to understand the value and impact of advanced resilient designs and operational excellence practices. Once they can understand and articulate the business case of cloud reliability engineering (CRE), they will be able to define and support resilience investment.

Summary

The ultimate goal of mature resilient practices is to build and maintain products that delight customers safely and efficiently while prioritizing and allocating engineering capacity based on their business needs. In this book, we will review multiple case studies from companies in technology, financial services, healthcare, and other industries so that you can review real-world examples (both successes and challenges) in implementing and maintaining resilient applications at an enterprise level.

Q&A

Q: Why are resilient designs important for companies large and small?

Resilience encompasses the practices, principles, and methodologies that ensure the availability, reliability, recovery, and efficiency of cloud-based systems. Through resilient designs, companies can unlock the full potential of the cloud and enhance their overall business performance.

Resilient designs enhance business continuity by maintaining seamless operations, even during unexpected failures or disruptions. Throughout this book, we will explore different aspects of building resilient applications, as well as stress-testing with chaos engineering where companies inject failures and disruptions to ensure the reliability of their systems.

Cloud resilience closely aligns with Lean and DevOps principles, fostering a culture of ownership comprising a "You build it, you own it" (YBYO) mentality, collaboration, and continuous improvements. This alignment empowers businesses to release high-quality software frequently, drive innovation, and respond quickly to market demands. It empowers people within these organizations to innovate on behalf of their customers.

Resilient designs are critical for the business and its customers in the following ways.

- For the business, it focuses on the optimization of cloud resources, automating operational tasks, and eliminating waste (one of the core Lean principles). It is costly to maintain cloud infrastructure, so optimizing cloud costs is of ultimate importance to every business. In this book, we will use AWS as an example of a partnership with your cloud provider in optimizing your costs.

- For customers, it plays a pivotal role in improving customer experience. Reliable cloud services enhance customer satisfaction and increase retention and Net Promoter Scores. They provide best practices to proactively identify and address potential issues to deliver a seamless, positive, and productive customer experience.

In summary, resilience engineering is a technical practice. It is of strategic importance to companies of all sizes, because it helps mitigate risk, optimize costs, drive innovation, grow the business, and deliver seamless and productive customer experiences leveraging the cloud and engineering.

Q: This all sounds great, but why should my company care about resilience engineering?

We're glad you are curious! Your company relies heavily on cloud-based services to serve your customers, and outages are your worst nightmare. You've probably experienced the frustration of trying to fix issues on the fly while your users are leaving for your competitors. Implementing resilience engineering is the key to keeping your cloud systems reliable, resilient, and secure. With resilient designs, your company will be equipped to tackle system outages head-on, with efficiency and finesse. Instead of reacting to incidents after they happen, your organization is empowered to proactively identify potential weaknesses in your cloud setup. It's like arming the organization with a super-sleuth magnifying glass to spot vulnerabilities and snuff them out before they become major problems or impact your customers and create potential reputational damage.

Resilience engineering is focused on continuous improvement where organizations embark on a journey of constant learning and optimization. Software development teams may conduct fun game days in which they simulate chaos and failures to test your system's resilience. This is like stress-testing your defenses to make sure they can handle anything the digital world throws at them. By eliminating wasteful processes and optimizing your cloud resources, your company will minimize its cloud costs. Many companies big and small are already reaping the benefits of resilient designs. Companies such as Netflix, Amazon, Capital One, Goldman Sachs, Airbnb, and Etsy have embraced well-architected principles to create robust, reliable, and customer-centric cloud systems. If companies do not care about resilience engineering, incidents are bound to happen.

Let's review some of the well-known examples of related incidents and their impact.

Google Cloud Service Disruption (June 2, 2019):

- **Type of outage:** Multiregion service disruption affecting GCP services and applications.
- **Timing:** The service disruption occurred during peak usage hours and persisted for several hours.
- **Impact:** Users experienced disruptions in accessing Google Cloud services, including Google Compute Engine (GCE), GKE, and Google Cloud Storage. Businesses relying on GCP for critical operations faced downtime and performance degradation.
- **Resolution:** Google engineers identified the root cause as an issue with the GCE network that led to connectivity problems. Remedial actions were taken to restore services and enhance network resilience.

Microsoft Azure Service Disruption (September 4, 2018):

- **Type of outage:** Global outage affecting Azure Active Directory authentication services.
- **Timing:** The service disruption occurred during business hours and lasted for several hours.
- **Impact:** Users reported issues with accessing various Microsoft services, including Office 365, Azure Portal, and Xbox Live, due to authentication failures.
- **Resolution:** Microsoft engineers traced the issue to a data center configuration error, which caused a spike in authentication requests and overwhelmed the system. Measures were implemented to prevent similar incidents and improve system resilience.

AWS S3 Service Disruption (February 28, 2017):

- **Type of outage:** Service disruption affecting Amazon S3 storage service in the US-EAST-1 region. Please note that in this case, the interruption was specific to a single region.
- **Timing:** The service disruption lasted for several hours and impacted a wide range of websites and services.
- **Impact:** Many popular websites and apps, including Airbnb, Netflix, and Reddit, experienced downtime or reduced functionality due to the inability to access S3 storage.
- **Resolution:** AWS engineers identified the root cause as an incorrect command entered during routine maintenance, which inadvertently took more servers offline than intended. Steps were taken to prevent similar incidents in the future.

The year 2017 was a banner year for service disruptions—and for the cost of them. Information Technology Intelligence Consulting's (ITIC) 2017 Cost of Downtime survey found that 98% of organizations say a single hour of downtime costs more than $100,000. More than 8 in 10 companies indicated that 60 minutes of downtime costs their business more than $300,000. A record one-third of enterprises reported that one hour of downtime costs their firms $1 million to more than $5 million. The average cost of a single hour of unplanned downtime has risen by 25% to 30% since 2008, when ITIC first began tracking these figures. As ITIC stated, "Each second and minute of server downtime and the associated mission-critical applications costs the business money and raises transactional operations and monetary risks. In the digital era of interconnected intelligent systems and networks, unplanned downtime of even a few minutes is expensive and disruptive and can reverberate across the entire ecosystem. This includes data centers; virtualized public, private, and hybrid clouds; remote work and learning environments, and the intelligent network edge."

Most of these outages were on-premises issues. As an example, 75,000 people were affected by the three-day British Airways (BA) system failure in the summer of 2017. BA lost an estimated $135 million due to that outage. The culprit turned out to be a faulty uninterruptable power supply (UPS) device. And that loss figure doesn't count the forever-gone trust of customers who will look elsewhere for transatlantic flights the next time they travel. BA of course wasn't alone for having suffered financially for having its systems down. Joining BA were United Airlines (200 flights delayed for 2.5 hours, thousands of passengers stranded or missed connections), Starbucks (could only accept cash payments in affected stores), Facebook (millions of users offline and tens of millions of ads not served during 2.5 hours of downtime), and WhatsApp (600 million users affected, 5 billion messages lost), according to a well-known 2020 Chaos Engineering Report.

In 2021, TechChannel reported that 44% of enterprises say hourly downtime costs surpass $1 million—with COVID-19, security hacks, and remote working as driving factors. As reported, "Enterprise downtime is now more expensive than ever: Some 44% of firms indicate that hourly downtime costs exceed $1 million to over $5 million, exclusive of any legal fees, fines or penalties. Additionally, 91% of organizations said a single hour of downtime that takes mission-critical server hardware and applications offline, averages over $300,000 due to lost business, productivity disruptions, and remediation efforts. Meanwhile, only 1% of organizations—mainly very small businesses with 50 or fewer employees—estimate that hourly downtime costs less than $100,000."

To summarize, if you care about delivering exceptional customer experiences, cutting down on costly service disruptions, and staying ahead of the competition, implementing engineering and AI strategies to build unshakable applications is a must in the ever-expanding cloud universe.

Chapter 2

Resilient, Available, and Scalable Systems

Ensuring That Applications Can Handle Failure in a Controlled Manner

Every system, application, or component must be designed to ensure a reliable and consistent experience. That is, even if an underlying component of a service fails, the full service will still work, and customers can complete transactions successfully and without disruption. This means the system is resilient to failure and performs in a way that is transparent for its customers—even when there is a total failure, a partial failure of a given component, or a downstream dependency.

Key Concepts

Organizations, enterprise leaders, and engineering teams who are thinking about building resilient solutions must spend some time understanding the foundational concepts of reliability, such as fault tolerance, high availability, scalability, recovery, and others, as described in the sections that follow.

Fault Tolerance

A **fault-tolerant** system is a system that works even when there is presence of a failure within an application, component, or dependency. It is a system that is designed to be "always on" and can withstand issues. For example, having two or more power supplies in a cloud infrastructure ensures that if one fails, the other one can generate the same supply of power to offer continuity without interruption of service. The measure of success in this case is binary: Either it works or it doesn't.

High Availability

A **highly available** application means the service is available to users most of the time, and it is permissible to have some amount of downtime. Availability is defined as a method to evaluate whether an application is functioning properly and can meet the requirements of your customers. Application availability in the cloud is determined based on performance indicators or service level indicators (SLIs) such as uptime and downtime, total number of successful transactions, application response time, and others.

Keeping track of system performance and SLIs is critically important as it will help engineering organizations determine how to architect applications and handle planned outages to minimize customer impact.

It is also important to know that measuring availability levels is different based on the use case or the criticality of the individual application. For example, failure of a hospital's medical equipment can have fatal consequences for patients, whereas the sudden failure of a car's brake system could lead to a potentially dangerous driving situation, and planned weekend downtime of a school's website likely would only result in a minor inconvenience for students and parents.

The purpose of building and operating reliable systems is to consider such scenarios and plan for them in advance. How your organization reacts to these scenarios depends on the specifics of your organization's goals, customer behaviors, and expectations. This is why measuring uptime availability is important.

Table 2.1 shows a standard list of downtime goals that must be discussed and agreed upon by product, business, and engineering leadership. It is worth noting that some of these cases will be sufficient by leveraging a single-region design, while other, more complex cases will require multiregion designs and higher cost.

Table 2.1
Standard Downtime Goals

Availability	Yearly Downtime	Description	Use Case
99%	3.65 days (or 87.6 hours)	This level of availability might be acceptable for noncritical applications with minimal impact on users. It's best suited for applications in which occasional downtime is tolerable and cost-effectiveness is a priority.	Personal blog or hobby website hosted on a single server; other non-business-critical services
99.9%	8 hours, 45 minutes, 57 seconds	This level of availability is suitable for applications that are important but can tolerate short periods of unavailability. While downtime is minimized compared to the previous level, it's still acceptable for applications in which occasional interruptions can be managed without significant consequences.	Small-business website; internal tool for employee use; non-business-critical services
99.95%	4 hours, 20 minutes, 49 seconds	This level of availability is for mission-critical applications that require extremely brief downtime. It is best suited for a multiregion scenario.	Investing; emergency services; gaming; banking
99.99%	52 minutes, 9 seconds	This level of availability is ideal for mission-critical applications that drive significant revenue or have a high impact on users. Achieving this level of availability typically involves hosting applications across multiple Availability Zones (AZs) within a single region, ensuring redundancy and fault tolerance. Applications at this level are expected to be highly reliable and resilient, with minimal tolerance for downtime as even brief outages can result in substantial losses or reputational damage.	E-commerce platforms; online banking systems; major social media platforms

(Continued)

Availability	Yearly Downtime	Description	Use Case
99.999%	5 minutes, 15 seconds	This level of availability is essential for mission-critical applications that drive significant revenue or have a high impact on users. Achieving this level of availability typically involves hosting applications within a single region but across multiple AZs, ensuring redundancy and fault tolerance. Systems at this level must be highly reliable and resilient, with minimal tolerance for downtime as even brief outages can lead to substantial financial losses or reputational damage.	Organizational-level online payment processing systems (e.g., banks, financial institutions)
99.9999%	31 seconds	This level of availability is extremely high and is reserved for ultra-critical systems in which even the slightest interruption can have severe consequences. Achieving this level of availability typically involves redundant systems deployed across multiple geographically dispersed regions, each with multiple AZs. These systems require meticulous planning, redundancy, and fault tolerance measures to ensure uninterrupted operation. The cost and complexity of achieving this level of availability are exceptionally high, but are necessary for applications in which human lives or significant financial stakes are at risk.	Aerospace navigation systems; life-critical medical equipment
99.99999%	3.2 seconds	This level of availability is suitable for highly specialized equipment or critical systems in which any interruption could jeopardize years of work. Achieving this level of availability requires an unparalleled level of redundancy, fault tolerance, and real-time monitoring. Systems at this level typically employ multiple layers of redundancy, including geographically dispersed data centers, redundant power supplies, network links, and hardware components. The cost and complexity associated with achieving this level of availability are extraordinarily high, often involving cutting-edge technology and continuous monitoring and maintenance.	Highly specialized scientific research equipment; deep-space exploration systems

(Continued)

Availability	Yearly Downtime	Description	Use Case
99.999999%	31.5 milliseconds	This level of availability is suitable for systems in which even the slightest interruption could have significant financial or security implications. Achieving this level of availability requires state-of-the-art infrastructure, real-time data replication, and failover mechanisms. Systems at this level are often designed with fault tolerance at every level, including hardware, software, and network components. The cost and complexity associated with achieving this level of availability are exceptionally high, involving continuous monitoring, redundancy, and rapid response capabilities.	Ultra-high-frequency trading platforms; national defense systems
99.9999999%	3.15 milliseconds	This level of availability is suitable for cutting-edge technology systems or critical infrastructure. Achieving this level of availability requires unprecedented levels of redundancy, fault tolerance, and security measures. Systems at this level are designed with multiple layers of protection, including redundant data centers, automated failover systems, and advanced security protocols. The cost and complexity associated with achieving this level of availability are astronomical, often requiring significant investment in research, development, and ongoing maintenance.	Quantum computing systems; nuclear reactor control systems

As you navigate the alternatives for uptime and architecture designs, take into account that existing routing components can monitor application health and regional health. Consider choosing between latency-based routing leveraging Route 53 and geolocation-based routing within a region using an application load balancer (ALB).

Latency-based routing with Route 53 is a scalable and highly available domain name system (DNS)–based traffic management technique offered by Amazon Web Services (AWS). This approach leverages the global network of AWS data centers to direct user requests to the AWS region with the lowest latency, thereby optimizing the user experience. With Route 53, incoming requests are automatically routed to the AWS region that provides the shortest network path, minimizing response times and ensuring efficient handling of requests. For instance, if a user on the East Coast of the United States accesses a service, Route 53 routes their request to the AWS region located closest to them in the eastern region of the country, reducing latency for that user. Similarly, a request from a user on the West Coast would be directed to the closest AWS region in the western region of the country.

Geolocation-based routing within the Application Load Balancer (ALB) is an approach used to route traffic within a specific geographic area or region to different sets of resources or components based on the location of the incoming request. This functionality is particularly useful when a service spans multiple geographic regions within a single AWS region. Configuring the ALB to consider the geographical origin of the incoming request enables it to intelligently route requests to different backend components located within the same region but optimized for that specific geographic area. For example, if a service operates across different cities within the same region, the ALB can direct incoming requests from each city to different backend resources or microservices tailored to handle workloads specific to that city. This routing method helps avoid latency issues that might arise when a single service is required to access various components located in different regions by processing all related workloads for a given request within the same region, thus optimizing performance and response times for end users.

To summarize, you would use latency-based routing with Route 53 when your service or application has a global user base spread across different continents or regions. If you have users accessing your service from various locations worldwide, latency-based routing can direct them to the nearest AWS region, minimizing latency and optimizing response times.

You would use geolocation-based routing within an ALB when your application operates in a single AWS region but serves users from different geographical areas within that region (e.g., different cities or states). It helps direct traffic within the region to specific backend components or microservices optimized for those geographic areas. Another use case is compliance based. In scenarios where data sovereignty or compliance regulations require certain operations or data processing to be confined within specific geographic boundaries, geolocation-based routing ensures that requests are processed within the designated region, meeting compliance needs.

Choosing between these methods often depends on the geographic distribution of your users, the structure of your application, compliance considerations, and the need for optimized performance. Latency-based routing targets global optimization, while geolocation-based routing within a region focuses on fine-tuning within specific geographic areas inside a region.

Service Level Indicators

SLIs can be calculated based on several factors, such as error rates, uptime availability, number of canary test executions, and others. It accounts for the percentage of time the service was available over some period (days, weeks, months, years). It shows the past performance of the service, and it represents what already happened, meaning that in some cases, customers have already been impacted.

Scalability

A scalable service can handle rapid changes to traffic volumes, workloads, and customer demand. A great benefit of the cloud are elastic services that allow engineers to expand service capacity either vertically or horizontally (see Figure 2.1).

Vertical scaling involves increasing capacity by adding more resources, such as CPU, disk, and memory, to a single host.

Horizontal scaling involves expanding the fleet of hosts in a distributed manner to support the higher demand of services at a given time in a timely fashion. In this scenario, the increase in load will also increase the number of sessions of a service. By distributing host instances across multiple AZs, horizontal scaling increases service performance, response time, and other major parameters. For this to work without major issues, services must be designed to support

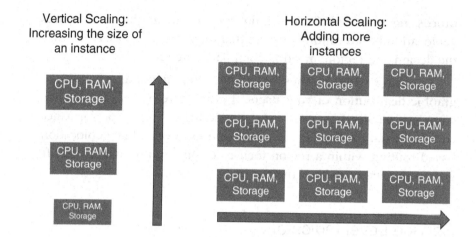

Figure 2.1
Vertical versus horizontal scaling

Vertical Scaling: Increasing the size of an instance

Horizontal Scaling: Adding more instances

a stateless scaling model, in which the service's state information is stored and requested independently from the host.

Organizations and engineering leaders must ensure that their systems are scalable by defining their requirements; choosing the right architecture based on uptime and downtime tolerances; implementing scaling techniques and related cloud services; and monitoring services to adapt to market changes. No system is static, and teams must assume that change in demand is expected.

To build and deploy scalable and reliable applications, engineering teams can leverage services offered by cloud providers. These services are ready to use within minutes, offer lots of benefits, and require simple configurations. Some design principles help achieve higher levels of resilience, such as serverless immutable infrastructure, loosely coupled implementations, and others. Let's review some of those.

"Application compute" refers to the hosts on which an application runs. Application compute must be elastic, that is, capable of increasing or decreasing to support different workloads based on seasonality, hours of the day, and major events such as Black Friday, Christmas, and the Super Bowl. With Amazon Elastic Compute Cloud (Amazon EC2), Auto Scaling groups (ASGs) help control capacity elastically, enabling application teams to monitor workload utilization and automate the addition or removal of resources to ensure that they meet the right levels of demand and capacity. Users can set a minimum number of instances, increments of instances based on capacity expectations or constraints (such as CPU usage), and a maximum capacity to ensure that costs are contained.

In tightly coupled implementations, a single server has a single database and a single point of failure, which makes it hard to recover from incidents in a timely fashion. In loosely coupled solutions, many AWS services and design patterns can help you create applications in a serverless and stateless fashion, which means if the workload fails, the system will repeatedly pick up workloads until it successfully ends processing. Figure 2.2 provides an example of the serverless architecture implemented using AWS services.

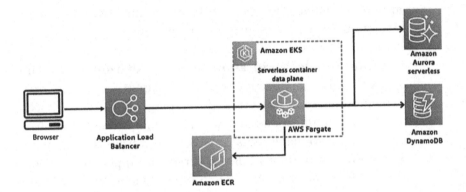

Figure 2.2
Example of a serverless microservices architecture (source: https://aws.amazon.com/blogs/architecture/architecting-for-reliable-scalability/; © 2024, Amazon Web Services, Inc.)

Immutable Infrastructure

Another concept to consider in your cloud implementation is immutable infrastructure. This is a model in which no updates, security patches, or configuration changes occur on production systems. If any change is needed, a new version of the stack is built and deployed into production. Mutable infrastructures allow for regular updates and modifications after the software has been deployed, whereas immutable infrastructures do not allow modifications once the software has been deployed.

Host images leveraging Amazon Machine Images (AMIs) are one example of this concept. AMIs are preconfigured templates for virtual machines (VMs) that include the operating system, application server, and applications. When using AMIs, any change to the infrastructure requires creating a new AMI and deploying it, rather than modifying an existing instance. Containers are also a good example of immutable infrastructure because persistent changes to containers can only be made by creating a new version of the container or re-creating the existing container from its image. AWS services such as AWS Cloud-Formation for infrastructure as code (IaC) and AWS Elastic Beanstalk for deploying and managing applications in a containerized environment facilitate this approach.

To support these design principles in an AWS environment, there are services to be considered: Amazon Simple Notification Service, Amazon Simple Queue Service, AWS Lambda, and AWS Step Functions, among others. Let's review them one by one.

- **Amazon Simple Notification Service (Amazon SNS):** This service allows application teams to capture requests from a queue and send out events leveraging other AWS services. SNS sends notifications and provides high-throughput, push-based, many-to-many messaging between distributed systems, microservices, and event-driven serverless applications. These applications include Amazon Simple Queue Service, AWS Lambda, and other HTTPS endpoints. It offers functionality that lets you send messages via SMS texts, push notifications, and email.
- **Amazon Simple Queue Service (Amazon SQS):** This is a fully managed message queuing service for microservices, distributed systems, and serverless applications. SQS enables you to send, store, and receive messages between software components at any volume, without losing messages or requiring other services to be available.
- **AWS Lambda:** This is a serverless, event-driven compute service that allows you to run code without thinking about servers or clusters. You can run code for virtually any type of application or backend service, without provisioning or managing servers. You can trigger Lambda from other AWS services and only pay for what you use.

- **AWS Step Functions:** This is a visual workflow service that helps developers use AWS services to build distributed applications, automate processes, orchestrate microservices, and create data and machine learning (ML) pipelines.

Let's dive deeper into event-driven architecture by leveraging a Lambda example and some best practices. When a function is triggered based on a given event, this is called an "invocation." A lambda function can be invoked to execute a piece of code without any infrastructure or costs associated with such an operation. There are three types of invocations.

- In a synchronous model, the client makes a request and waits for a response.
- In an asynchronous model, the client sends a request and may get an acknowledgment that the event was received, but it doesn't get a response that includes the results of the request.
- In a polling event, consumers poll the producer for messages in batches and then process the batch before returning for a new batch of records.

Figure 2.3 illustrates event-driven architecture leveraging a lambda function. This architecture allows you to combine serverless, event-driven components to build highly scalable and efficient workflows. By using EventBridge, Amazon Simple Storage Service (Amazon S3), and AWS Lambda together, you can handle complex data processing, automate scheduled tasks, and integrate with other AWS services seamlessly.

Load Balancing

To prepare and manage customer traffic, engineering teams need to introduce the concept of load balancing. AWS offers ALBs and network load balancers (NLBs). A load balancer serves as the single point of contact for clients. The ALB distributes incoming application traffic across multiple targets, such as EC2 instances, in multiple AZs. This increases the availability of your application. The NLB allows

Figure 2.3
Event-driven architecture example (source: https://aws.amazon.com/blogs/compute/operating-lambda-understanding-event-driven-architecture-part-1/; © 2024, Amazon Web Services, Inc.)

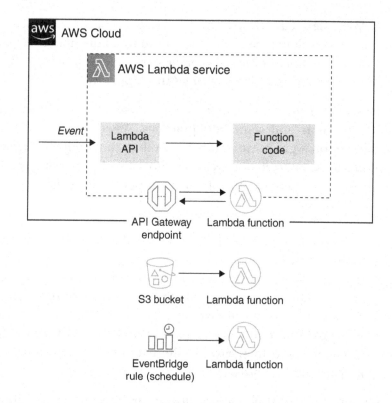

you to balance and route traffic by using the TCP/IP networking protocol. Load balancing distributes request processing across multiple servers or endpoints, and a failover redirects requests to alternative servers if the originally requested server is unavailable or too slow.

Recovery

Recovery is also essential for organizations and engineering leaders. It is not enough to think about *whether* a system will go down; you must assume it *will* go down. Therefore, it is imperative to know how application teams will react to those scenarios well in advance. Preparing for incidents with the right playbooks and preparing for different types of incidents can be the difference between a minor incident that is fixed internally without impacting the customer and an incident that ends up damaging your company's reputation and possibly its revenues.

Following are examples of incidents.

- With loads that are too big, your system can break or degrade the experience offered to your customers. In this case, you need to focus on elasticity and scalability.
- Attacks can sometimes be caused accidentally by your application (e.g., a bug introduced during development). In this case, you need to think about high availability. Sometimes these attacks can be malicious (e.g., an attacker trying to penetrate your application data or take some components down), so you need to think about security and incident response.
- Component failures that are critical dependencies for your main service can also fail. In this case, you need to consider design patterns and architectures to isolate issues when your dependencies are down.

Incident response and recovery is an important and broad topic. For more information, see Chapter 3, "Incident Response for Fast Recovery: How to Handle Incidents and How to Automate This Process to Improve Time to Detect and Time to Recovery."

Design Principles

In the cloud, incidents can be prevented by leveraging design principles and architectures. For example, when you service the same components in multiple AZs within a single region, and one component fails in a single AZ, your system will be able to respond to customer requests in alternate AZs.

Depending on the business objectives and criticality of the application, you can implement the application in multiple AZs and multiple regions to ensure resilience based on geolocation. For example, having an active-active stack in the west and east regions of a country offers geolocation-based resilience, giving you a chance to automatically (based on health checks) reroute traffic to the stack in the west region if the stack in the east region is down.

While regions and AZs are fundamental concepts in cloud computing, their implementation can vary across different cloud providers. AWS defines "regions" as the separate geographical locations around the world where the company has data centers. Each region is completely independent and isolated from the others, meaning that if one region experiences an outage, it does not affect the others. AWS currently has multiple regions globally, including in North America, Europe, Asia Pacific, and more. Within each AWS region, there are multiple AZs. An AZ is essentially a separate data center within the same region, but each AZ is isolated from the others, with its own power, cooling, and networking infrastructure. This isolation ensures that if one AZ experiences a failure, the others remain unaffected, providing high availability and fault tolerance.

While AWS popularized the concept of regions and AZs, other cloud providers may have different terminology or implementations for similar concepts. AWS's definition and approach are widely regarded as effective and advantageous due to their clear isolation, redundancy, scalability, and consistency.

Chaos Engineering

Now that you have leveraged the basic design principles and used the AWS services to ensure that your systems, applications, and services are reliable, it is time to confirm that your systems can handle failure in a controlled manner by introducing failure in your production environment to identify how those applications will respond to it. This is what we introduced in Chapter 1 as "chaos engineering." It is a practice that needs to happen constantly to create a culture of operational excellence and to prevent issues before customers experience them. Ideal scenarios will be tested first in QA or in a nonprod environment to ensure the validity of the test (also known as a "hypothesis"), and then in production to minimize impacting customers unnecessarily.

The ultimate goal is to design applications, test them automatically via chaos engineering game days, and ensure that your organization is ready to execute all these practices in a disaster recovery scenario. Ultimately, the assumption is that any system will fail at some point, so the question is not whether it will happen, but when it will happen and how you will react to it. Considering and testing different disaster recovery scenarios is the primary mechanism to ensure that your organization's systems will be healthy when a real case hits. Think about what steps you will take when compute is in trouble, when your database goes down, when one of the AZs or regions is impacted, when your app teams introduce errors in the code, and other possible scenarios, and devise your responses to each of these situations.

Validating Resilience

Leading cloud providers offer guidelines on how to validate the resilience of their applications and infrastructure against various failure scenarios. For example, the AWS Fault Injection Simulator (FIS) provides a comprehensive guide on creating and managing experiment templates. AWS FIS enables users to easily create and execute experiments to validate the resilience of their applications and infrastructure against various failure scenarios. The experiment templates serve as predefined configurations that specify the parameters, actions, and targets for conducting experiments. By utilizing experiment templates, users can streamline the process of setting up and executing experiments as well as ensuring consistency and repeatability across different testing scenarios.

The stages for managing an experiment are as follows.

1. **Introduction to experiment templates:** Provide an overview of what experiment templates are and their significance in the context of the AWS FIS.
2. **Accessing experiment templates:** Guide readers on how to access the experiment templates provided by AWS FIS.
3. **Understanding experiment template components:** Explain the different components of an experiment template, including parameters, actions, and targets.

4. **Creating experiment templates:** Walk users through the process of creating custom experiment templates tailored to their specific testing requirements.

5. **Managing experiment templates:** Discuss how to manage and organize experiment templates effectively within the AWS FIS console.

6. **Executing experiments using templates:** Demonstrate how to execute experiments using the predefined templates, showcasing their versatility and ease of use.

7. **Analyzing experiment results:** Highlight the importance of analyzing experiment results to gain insights into system behavior and resilience.

8. **Iterative improvement:** Encourage readers to iterate on their experiment templates based on findings and observations from previous experiments, fostering a culture of continuous improvement in resilience testing practices.[1]

Microsoft Azure provides a Resiliency Checklist containing a comprehensive set of guidelines and best practices to enhance the resilience of cloud-based services.

In addition, Google Cloud includes resilience in its set of patterns and practices for creating scalable and resilient apps, emphasizing the importance of careful planning and design to achieve the following goals.

- **Scalability**
  a. Scalability refers to a system's ability to handle varying workloads by adjusting resources.
  b. Well-designed apps scale up or down based on demand, ensuring optimal performance and cost-effectiveness.
  c. Google Cloud offers products such as Compute Engine, Kubernetes Engine, and serverless options for efficient resource management and cost optimization.

---

1. For detailed information on AWS FIS experiment templates, refer to the official AWS documentation available at https://docs.aws.amazon.com/fis/latest/userguide/experiment-templates.html.

- **Resilience**
  a. Resilient apps continue to function despite failures of system components.
  b. Resilience requires planning at all architecture levels, including infrastructure layout, app design, and organizational culture.
  c. Google Cloud provides tools and services such as regional availability, load balancing, and managed compute/database products for building highly available and resilient apps.
- **Drivers and constraints**
  a. Various drivers, including business, development, and operational needs, motivate the improvement of scalability and resilience.
  b. Constraints such as hardware dependencies, licensing restrictions, and organizational resistance may limit scalability and resilience efforts.
- **Patterns and practices**
  a. Automation is crucial for building scalable and resilient apps, reducing human error, and increasing speed.
  b. Loose coupling, that is, treating systems as collections of independent components, enhances flexibility and resilience.
  c. Data-driven design, in which metrics and logs are utilized to understand app behavior, informs scaling decisions and service health assessments.
- **Automation and IaC**
  a. Automate infrastructure provisioning to enhance consistency and reproducibility of environments.
  b. Treat infrastructure provisioning as code, enabling versioning, auditing, and integration with CI/CD pipelines.
  c. Google Cloud offers tools such as Cloud Deployment Manager and Config Connector, as well as support for third-party IaC tools such as Terraform, Chef, and Puppet.
- **Immutable infrastructure**
  a. Immutable infrastructure ensures that resources are never modified after deployment, promoting predictability and mitigating configuration drift.

b. Updates are made by redeploying resources with updated configurations from the source repository.

c. This approach reduces issues common in mutable infrastructures, such as configuration drift and snowflake servers.

- **High availability**
  a. High availability aims to maximize service availability through redundancy and distribution of components.

  b. Google Cloud's global infrastructure allows the distribution of resources across regions and zones to enhance availability and resilience.

  c. Managed services such as Cloud SQL provide built-in redundancy and manage data replication and backups, reducing the need for manual intervention.

  d. Load balancing distributes traffic among resources to prevent overloads and ensure optimal performance.

- **Monitoring infrastructure and apps**
  a. Comprehensive monitoring provides insight into the health and performance of your application.

  b. Cloud Monitoring in Google Cloud offers integrated monitoring, ingesting events, metrics, and metadata to provide insights through dashboards and alerts.

  c. Monitoring should occur at all levels, including infrastructure, app, service, and end to end.

- **Exposing app health**
  a. Implementing health checks allows systems to determine the health of various components and route requests accordingly.

  b. Load balancers typically handle health checks, but Kubernetes also supports liveness and readiness probes for app health monitoring.

- **Defining key metrics and service level objectives (SLOs)**
  a. Key metrics such as latency, traffic, errors, and saturation help monitor the health and performance of user-facing systems.

  b. SLOs specify target levels of performance or reliability for services, allowing teams to measure and maintain service quality.

- **Storage and database technology**
  a. Choose appropriate databases and storage technologies based on scalability, availability, and consistency requirements.
  b. NoSQL databases offer increased availability and scalability but may sacrifice some features of relational databases.
- **Scaling profile and deployment automation**
  a. Balancing cost and user experience is crucial when deciding on scaling profiles and deployment strategies.
  b. Auto-scaling and optimization techniques, such as prebaked images and containerization, help ensure efficient scaling and deployment.
- **Modernizing development processes**
  a. DevOps practices promote agility and reduced time to market by breaking down silos between development, operations, and related teams.
  b. Testability, automated testing, deployment automation, and incident management are key aspects of modern development practices.
- **Testing and validating architecture**
  a. Testing resilience and scaling behavior is essential to ensure that applications behave as expected under varying conditions.
  b. Continuous refinement and adaptation of architectures is necessary to keep pace with evolving technology and user demands.

Summary

By following well-thought-out strategies, organizations can build and maintain resilient, scalable, and efficient cloud-native applications while fostering a culture of continuous improvement and innovation.

Q&A

Q: What is chaos engineering and how do I stress-test my cloud apps?

If your goal is to build reliable and resilient systems, the best way to test them is to introduce chaos: a variety of different disturbances. Chaos engineering tests the systems by introducing unexpected failures, disruptions, network failures, software bugs—anything that can disrupt normal function. Imagine a banking application. What happens if a network server fails in the middle of a money transfer? It won't be good if a person using the banking application loses funds because the transaction was not complete. What if a gamer is in the middle of a game and the network connection becomes slow because of high network traffic? Chaos engineering tests such scenarios to ensure that the server infrastructure is robust enough to handle required functionality despite all possible challenges, and identifies vulnerabilities that need to be addressed.

Possible approaches include latency injection simulating slow network traffic, stress testing simulating an abnormally high number of connections, server failure simulating specific servers shutting down at random intervals, or database load testing simulating huge queries being executed, jamming the database.

Chaos engineering experiments can be executed in the following phases: prepare, assess, analyze, score, and remediate, as illustrated in Figure 2.4.

In each instance, you must focus on the most important areas to address possible failures and disruptions. Once you determine the most critical components of the system that are essential for its proper functioning, you need to set up the hypothesis about how the system might fail under specific conditions, and then simulate these conditions. Next, you need to monitor system behavior and analyze and collect data to identify any failures, anomalies, and performance issues. Scoring is a technique to evaluate the impact of chaos engineering experiments.

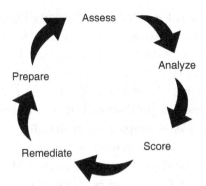

Figure 2.4
Chaos engineering
phases

During scoring, you evaluate the impact of the chaos experience from the point of severity, impact, probability of failure, risk, and other relevant parameters. Finally, you remediate the issue by fixing bugs, updating configurations, changing application architecture, optimizing processes, and taking other measures to eliminate the root cause for any vulnerabilities that impact the system.

From a cloud reliability engineering (CRE) perspective, chaos engineering requires continuous improvement. You cannot run chaos engineering experiments once, fix the issues found, and forget about it. New disruptions in security, software, and hardware are introduced daily. It is important to iterate and improve your system by rerunning chaos experiments to address any new potential vulnerabilities. Most importantly, any chaos experiments should not have a negative impact on your user experience, so stage these experiments in a thoughtful and structured way.

Q: What is a game day?

Game days simulate failures to test systems, processes, and people's responses. Doing this helps organizations understand where improvements can be made and develop organizational experience in dealing with major incidents in production. The suggested approach is to conduct these regularly so that application teams build muscle memory on how to triage, act, and measure during highly stressful situations.

After your design for resiliency, the initial step is to test in non-production environments; a game day is the way to ensure that everything works as planned in production. If a negative impact is observed, the game day test is rolled back and the workload issues are remedied, manually if necessary (using the runbook). Since game days often take place in production, all precautions should be taken to ensure that there is no impact on availability to your customers. It is also imperative to have a centralized tool, catalog of experiments, and team-to-run game days. In organizations with thousands of applications, symptoms of failure can be created in different applications from core dependencies, and not knowing when a game day is happening can cause loss of time and energy from teams trying to understand what is happening without realizing it is a test. This will be similar to having an airport that allows airplanes to land without the proper authorization; at some point there will be a crash, creating devastating results for the organization and impacting its customers.

Q: What is a Chaos Service Catalog, and what are some of the most common failure scenarios?

A Chaos Service Catalog is a centralized repository where various experiments, simulations, and hypotheses related to system resilience and failure scenarios are stored and managed. It's a crucial resource used in chaos engineering practices to deliberately introduce controlled failures into a system to assess its resiliency and identify weaknesses before they become critical issues.

Here's an expansion on the mentioned failure scenarios.

- **Disabling hosts for capacity reflection:** Simulating reduced capacity by intentionally disabling specific hosts or instances within a system. This helps in understanding how the system responds when resources become limited and how it manages load distribution.

- **AZ network service disruption:** Creating a scenario in which one or more AZs lose network connectivity. This test allows evaluation of the system's ability to handle a network service disruption within specific zones and how it reroutes traffic to maintain functionality.
- **Errors in monitoring systems:** Introducing deliberate errors or faults into monitoring systems to assess how well the system detects, reports, and responds to anomalies or faults in monitoring data.
- **Disconnecting an entire virtual private cloud (VPC):** Simulating the disconnection or isolation of an entire VPC to evaluate the system's resilience when the entire network infrastructure is disrupted.
- **Failover using inactive stack:** Triggering a failover operation using the most recent inactive stack or configuration to test the failover process and assess its reliability.
- **Bypassing multifactor authentication (MFA):** Testing the system's dependency on MFA by deliberately bypassing it. This helps identify components or systems that rely solely on MFA and might become nonoperational without it.
- **AWS ECS task actions:** Testing fault injection actions that target Amazon AWS ECS workloads including CPU stress, I/O stress, killing certain processes, discarding network traffic, or simulating a network packet loss.

These scenarios represent intentional disruptions or failures introduced in a controlled environment to understand how a system reacts and recovers from such events. Through these simulations, organizations can proactively identify weaknesses, strengthen their systems, and improve overall resilience.

AWS provides a helpful example of a power interruption scenario as a means to simulate the effects of a complete interruption of power in an AZ. This scenario aims to validate the resilience of multi-AZ applications during a single, complete AZ power outage. It encompasses various symptoms such as loss of zonal compute, subnet connectivity loss, Amazon Relational Database Service (RDS) failover, ElastiCache failover, and unresponsive Elastic Block

Store (EBS) volumes. The actions involved in this scenario include stopping instances, stopping AWS ASG instances, pausing instance launches, pausing ASG scaling, pausing network connectivity, failover of RDS, pausing Amazon ElastiCache Redis, and pausing Amazon EBS I/O. Each action targets specific resources and components affected by the power interruption. Limitations of the scenario are also outlined, such as the absence of stop conditions and unsupported configurations like Amazon EKS Pods running on AWS Fargate. This scenario serves as a valuable tool for assessing and enhancing the resilience of applications and infrastructure in the face of unexpected disruptions.

Q: What are the most common chaos anti-patterns?

Following are some common chaos engineering anti-patterns and dependency issues.

- **Overemphasizing chaos, while ignoring the basics:** Focusing solely on chaos engineering without ensuring foundational reliability practices. It's crucial to have solid monitoring, incident response, and stability before introducing chaos experiments.
- **Chaos experiments without safety nets:** Conducting chaos experiments without proper safeguards or without considering potential impacts on critical services. Lack of isolation or safeguards can lead to widespread disruptions.
- **Inadequate experiment scoping:** Running overly broad or untargeted chaos experiments that affect more systems than necessary. Narrowly scoped experiments help identify specific weaknesses without unnecessary disruptions.
- **Static chaos planning:** Relying on fixed, predictable chaos scenarios. Chaos engineering should evolve with the system, introducing variability in experiments to simulate real-world conditions.

- **Ignoring dependencies in chaos experiments:** Overlooking dependencies or coupling between systems when designing chaos experiments. This can lead to chaos-induced cascading failures that aren't reflective of real-world scenarios.
- **Ineffective recovery time objective (RTO) validation:** Relying solely on CI/CD pipelines and tools for RTO validations, which might not accurately represent real-world recovery scenarios, leading to a false sense of security. Companies must consider running all pipelines at the same time or not having a CI/CD pipeline tooling (e.g., Jenkins) available during an incident.
- **Excessive disruption to production:** Conducting chaos experiments in a live production environment without appropriate control or abort mechanisms. This can lead to customer impact and degrade user experience.
- **Lack of collaboration and learning:** Failing to involve all stakeholders (developers, operations, etc.) or not sharing learnings from chaos experiments across the organization. This inhibits collective learning and improvement.

To mitigate these anti-patterns, it's essential to focus on thoughtful experimentation, starting with small, controlled scenarios, considering system dependencies, and fostering a culture of learning and collaboration around chaos engineering practices. Validating RTOs in a way that mirrors real system behavior and using chaos experiments as a learning tool rather than a disruptor can significantly improve system reliability.

Q: How to test recovery procedures and playbooks?

Recovery procedures and playbooks require thorough testing for each scenario, process, and best practice. From a Lean perspective, you need to focus on minimizing waste, maximizing value, and establishing continuous improvement while introducing measures to ensure compliance with the playbooks and recovery procedures specified for each system.

This is done in several phases. First, we need to ensure that objectives are well stated and there is a shared understanding of success criteria. Success criteria are primarily quantitative. Some of the parameters to consider include the RTOs, recovery point objectives (RPOs), and system availability data, or uptime, as discussed in this chapter. Second, we need to establish phases and boundaries for the experiments and automate testing so that test results are repeatable and reliable. Then, we run tests in a sequence and/or in batches, measure outcomes, and document and share learnings.

Two Lean principles become highly important in this process:

- Continuous improvement (Kaizen), which allows leveraging the Lean philosophy of continuous improvement to review and refine the playbooks and recovery procedures
- Frequent feedback loops, allowing us to capture the feedback from stakeholders and end users based on each experiment

Q: How to measure reliability?

This is a great question—and we thought you'd never ask! CRE is data and fact driven. One of the most important questions that every organization needs to answer is: How do we measure CRE parameters such as resilience and reliability, and how do we benchmark them against industry standards?

There is no one-size-fits-all answer here. Think of it as a restaurant menu. Say you are at The Cheesecake Factory, and you're handed a huge menu comprising several pages of items, most of which sound tasty. However, you can't afford to eat all of those simultaneously—at least, not if you want to stay healthy. In the first question in this section, we discussed chaos engineering when we need to define the most important parameters to measure and focus on while simulating failures in a controlled environment.

Similarly, there are many parameters that we may want to measure in this scenario.

- SLOs and SLIs, which reflect the desired reliability and resilience of our cloud services. These may include uptime, response time, error rates, and other relevant parameters. For example, an SLI might be "99.9% availability in a year."
- Error budget, which represents the allowable amount of downtime or errors a service can experience while still meeting its SLOs. You can set up an error budget of one hour of downtime per month, which means your service would meet reliability targets even if its downtime was less than one hour per month.
- Mean time between failures (MTBF), which measures the average time between failures, and mean time to recover (MTTR), which measures the average time it takes to recover from a failure. Both metrics are essential for understanding the reliability and resilience of your cloud applications. A lower MTTR and a higher MTBF indicate better performance.

There are multiple other metrics, such as incident response metrics to evaluate the efficiency of your incident response process using such parameters as time to detect issues, time to acknowledge, and time to fix; or business impact analysis, allowing you to consider the impact of failures on business objectives and customer experiences. There is no limit to what you can measure depending on where your business bottleneck is and what data is available.

It is important to review your metrics regularly and monitor and refine the data you are collecting, to ensure that there are no blind spots in defining the metrics for you to collect on an ongoing basis and in displaying the data on live dashboards or sharing a regular report. From a Lean values–driven perspective, you need to start by considering the specific requirements and goals of your organization when defining these measurements.

Chapter 3

Incident Response for Fast Recovery

How to Handle Incidents and How to Automate This Process to Improve Time to Detect and Time to Recovery

"Fast recovery" in cloud reliability engineering (CRE) refers to the set of practices, procedures, and tools employed by organizations to effectively manage and mitigate the impact of incidents or disruptions in their cloud-based applications. These practices aim to minimize downtime, data loss, and customer impact while ensuring the speedy recovery of services.

Incident Response

First, let us define incident response. Incident response involves the structured approach taken by teams to detect, triage, and respond to failures promptly. It includes seven steps:

Step 1.   Detection
Step 2.   Analysis
Step 3.   Containment

Step 4.   Mitigation

Step 5.   Resolution

Step 6.   Communication

Step 7.   Documentation

The sections that follow describe these steps in further detail.

Step 1: Detection

This step involves identifying issues or incidents through monitoring, alerting, and anomaly detection systems.

To effectively detect incidents, organizations deploy a combination of real-time monitoring tools that continuously observe system metrics, application performance, and key operational parameters. These tools generate alerts when predefined thresholds or anomalies are detected, which helps teams identify deviations from normal operations. In the context of CRE, the emphasis is on keeping detection processes lean and efficient. This means monitoring should be focused on key performance indicators (KPIs) that directly impact user experience and system stability. By carefully selecting and fine-tuning monitoring criteria, CRE teams minimize noise and false positives, ensuring that alerts are meaningful and actionable.

Furthermore, CRE encourages a data-driven approach to detection. By leveraging historical data and performance baselines, organizations can establish more accurate thresholds for anomaly detection, allowing them to spot unusual behavior with greater precision.

Step 2: Analysis

This step involves assessing the severity and scope of the incident to understand its impact on customers and systems.

During this phase, CRE teams gather and analyze relevant data to assess the incident's severity. This involves examining the incident's characteristics, its potential impact on customers, and the affected systems or services. The goal is to quickly establish a clear understanding of the incident's scope, pinpointing whether it's localized to a specific component or has broader implications across the infrastructure, also known as the "blast radius." CRE teams rely on data-driven insights, historical incident records, and predefined incident response plans to expedite this analysis. By evaluating the severity accurately, organizations can prioritize their incident response efforts effectively, ensuring that resources are allocated where they are needed most and that notifications to senior leadership, risk, or regulatory teams are escalated appropriately. This process must be predefined, validated against a preestablished severity matrix during the incident, and free from ambiguity, thus accelerating the engagement approach, communications, and other critical response actions.

Step 3: Containment

This step involves isolating affected systems or components to prevent further damage or disruption.

During this phase, CRE teams employ predefined strategies and protocols to isolate the affected systems or components. This might involve temporarily disabling certain services, rerouting traffic, or implementing access controls to prevent unauthorized access to compromised areas. The primary objective is to create a controlled environment to minimize the incident's impact and reduce or prevent additional harm. Containment strategies are designed to strike a balance between safeguarding the overall system's integrity and maintaining essential services, ensuring that user experience is not unduly disrupted.

Effective containment practices in CRE are characterized by a rapid response, clear communication, and the utilization of automation where possible. The goal is to halt the incident's progression while allowing incident response teams to work on resolution without the burden of further system degradation. Additionally, containment measures may include real-time monitoring and ongoing assessment to ensure that the incident remains isolated and does not escalate. By efficiently executing the containment step, organizations can reduce downtime, customer impact, and potential financial losses while moving closer to incident resolution.

Step 4: Mitigation

This step involves implementing short-term solutions or workarounds to minimize the impact on customers.

Mitigation strategies in CRE focus on identifying the most pressing aspects of the incident and swiftly applying solutions that can reduce their impact. These solutions are often considered temporary measures, and their primary goal is to restore service functionality or, at the very least, maintain service availability while further investigation and resolution efforts continue.

For example, if an incident affects a critical application, mitigation might involve rerouting traffic to redundant servers, disabling specific features to reduce the load, or implementing failover mechanisms to ensure uninterrupted service. It's crucial to prioritize these actions based on the severity of the incident and its impact on users.

Mitigation in CRE should align with predefined incident response plans and procedures, usually defined in playbooks, to allow for a structured and efficient approach. Moreover, communication remains a key element during this phase, ensuring that stakeholders are informed about the actions being taken and any potential changes to the user experience. Successful mitigation efforts not only alleviate the immediate impact but also buy time for the incident response teams to identify the root cause and work on a more permanent resolution.

Step 5: Resolution

This step involves identifying the root cause and implementing long-term fixes to prevent recurrence.

Resolution in CRE requires a meticulous investigation into the incident's cause, often involving cross-functional collaboration among engineering teams, developers, and relevant stakeholders. The objective is not just to patch up the immediate problem but also to understand why it happened (i.e., determine the root cause) and how to prevent similar issues going forward. This might involve code reviews, system architecture assessments, and in-depth analysis of logs and performance data. Once the root cause is identified, comprehensive solutions and improvements are designed and tested to address it effectively. These solutions might involve code changes, infrastructure adjustments, or updates to operational procedures, depending on the nature of the incident.

CRE emphasizes the importance of not just fixing the problem but also learning from it to build a more resilient system. This phase involves documenting lessons learned, updating incident response plans, and continuously improving processes to enhance overall system reliability. The goal is to ensure that similar incidents are less likely to occur in the future, contributing to a culture of continuous improvement and reliability within the organization.

Step 6: Communication

This step involves keeping stakeholders informed about the incident's status and expected resolution time.

During this phase, the incident response team provides regular updates to stakeholders, including internal teams, leadership, and sometimes external customers/users if the incident impacts them. These updates should include the current status of the incident, the actions being taken to resolve it, and estimated timelines for resolution. Communication should be clear, concise, and tailored to the audience, ensuring that technical details are explained in a way that nontechnical stakeholders can understand.

Moreover, CRE emphasizes proactive and continuous communication throughout the incident's lifecycle. This involves not only providing updates when there are significant developments, but also acknowledging receipt of reports, setting expectations for regular updates, and ensuring that stakeholders are aware of any changes in the situation. This transparent and collaborative approach fosters a culture of accountability, trust, and shared responsibility for maintaining system reliability. It also helps prevent speculation and misinformation, enabling stakeholders to make informed decisions and respond effectively to the incident.

Step 7: Documentation

This step involves recording all details related to the incident for post-incident analysis and learning.

During this phase, the incident response team compiles a comprehensive incident report that includes a detailed timeline of events, the actions taken to mitigate and resolve the incident, the root cause analysis (RCA) findings, and any recommendations for preventive measures. It's crucial to capture both technical and nontechnical aspects of the incident, as well as the impact on users, systems, and the organization as a whole. The documentation should be clear, structured, and easily accessible to relevant stakeholders.

In addition, CRE emphasizes the importance of conducting a **post-incident review or retrospective meeting**, where the incident response team and other relevant parties come together to analyze the incident in depth and in a blameless mode. This retrospective aims to identify what worked well during the incident response, what could have been handled better, and what systemic improvements can be made to prevent similar incidents in the future. It's a valuable learning opportunity that aligns with Lean principles of continuous improvement and empowers teams to adapt and evolve their practices for greater reliability and resilience. We will discuss it in detail in Chapter 4, "Operational Excellence and Change Management: How to Establish Efficient Processes and Maintain Best-in-Class CRE Practices."

Fast Recovery

Fast recovery in CRE emphasizes the need for quick restoration of services and systems following an incident. It involves strategies and tools implemented in the following seven steps:

Step 1. Minimize downtime
Step 2. Restore data
Step 3. Automate recovery
Step 4. Implement redundancy
Step 5. Test and validate
Step 6. Prioritize customer experience
Step 7. Pursue continuous improvement

The sections that follow describe these steps in further detail.

Step 1: Minimize Downtime

This step involves reducing the duration during which services are unavailable to customers. This step is fundamentally aligned with Lean principles of eliminating waste and maximizing efficiency. When an incident occurs, minimizing downtime becomes critical not only to maintain customer trust but also to ensure the organization's operational efficiency.

To achieve this, CRE teams employ strategies such as automated failover mechanisms, load balancing, and rapid response protocols. For example, they may implement auto-scaling to dynamically adjust resource capacity based on real-time demand, ensuring that there are sufficient resources available to handle increased traffic or load spikes. Additionally, they often use deployment practices such as canary releases or blue-green deployments (these are discussed in more detail in Chapter 7, "CRE Tooling: Tools That Support Automatic Failovers, Automatic Rollbacks, Automatic Deployments, Chaos Engineering, Incident Response, Configuration Management, Immutable Infrastructure, and Disaster Recovery"), allowing them to roll out updates or changes with minimal impact on ongoing services. App teams can also leverage feature flags to turn features on and off while the problem is addressed or a fix is in place. The key is to proactively design systems and processes that can swiftly adapt to disruptions, ensuring that downtime is kept to an absolute minimum.

Furthermore, CRE encourages a culture of continuous improvement, where incident response teams conduct post-incident analyses to identify opportunities for further minimizing downtime in the future. This aligns with Lean's principles of relentless pursuit of efficiency and waste reduction. By continuously refining incident response processes and optimizing system architectures, organizations can progressively reduce downtime and enhance the reliability of their services, ultimately delivering a better experience for users.

Step 2: Restore Data

This step involves ensuring that data remains consistent and available, preventing data loss.

Data is a critical asset for organizations, and any disruption or loss can have severe consequences. CRE teams prioritize strategies that allow for rapid data recovery and minimal data loss during incidents. To achieve this, organizations implement practices such as frequent data backups, data replication across multiple Availability Zones (AZs) or regions, and real-time synchronization mechanisms. For example, they might use services such as the following.

- **AWS S3 Data Replication:** This service allows organizations to replicate data across multiple AWS regions, ensuring high availability and durability. In the event of a regional outage or failure, data remains accessible from other regions, minimizing downtime and data loss.
- **AWS RDS Multi-AZ:** With Multi-AZ deployment, Amazon Relational Database Service (RDS) automatically replicates data to a standby instance in a different AZ. In the event of a failure in one zone, traffic is automatically redirected to the standby

instance, ensuring continuous availability and minimal disruption to operations.

- **Google Cloud Storage Nearline and Coldline:** Google Cloud offers nearline and coldline storage classes for data backup and archival, providing cost-effective options for storing infrequently accessed data with low latency retrieval. By leveraging these storage classes, organizations can ensure data redundancy and availability while optimizing storage costs.

- **Google Cloud Spanner:** Google Cloud Spanner provides globally distributed, horizontally scalable relational database service with strong consistency and high availability. It automatically replicates data across multiple regions and zones, ensuring resilience against regional outages and minimizing data loss.

- **Microsoft Azure Backup:** Azure Backup offers cloud-based backup solutions for protecting data across Azure services, on-premises environments, and hybrid deployments. It supports automated backups with incremental backups and backup retention policies, enabling organizations to recover data quickly and efficiently in the event of data loss or corruption.

- **Microsoft Azure SQL Database Geo-Replication:** Azure SQL Database offers geo-replication capabilities to replicate data across multiple Azure regions for high availability and disaster recovery. By replicating data asynchronously to secondary databases in different regions, organizations can ensure data redundancy and minimize downtime during regional outages.

Additionally, disaster recovery planning involves defining recovery point objectives (RPOs) and recovery time objectives (RTOs) for different data types and systems. CRE emphasizes the importance of regular testing and validation of data recovery processes to ensure that they meet these objectives.

CRE also recognizes that data restoration is not a one-time activity but an ongoing commitment to data reliability. It involves continuous monitoring of data integrity, automated failover mechanisms, and proactive detection of potential data inconsistencies. By combining these practices with efficient data recovery strategies, organizations can minimize data loss and maintain data consistency, even in the face of unexpected incidents, aligning with Lean principles of continuous improvement and waste reduction.

Step 3: Automate Recovery

This step involves leveraging automation to expedite the recovery process and reduce manual intervention. Automation is a key principle of CRE, aiming to reduce human error, save time, and ensure consistent and efficient responses to incidents. To achieve automated recovery, organizations implement scripts, playbooks, automated runbooks, and workflows that can quickly detect incidents and trigger predefined recovery procedures. For example, they might use the following tools and services.

- **AWS lambda functions combined with AWS CloudWatch alarms:** Organizations can set up lambda functions to respond automatically to events detected by CloudWatch alarms. For instance, if CPU utilization exceeds a certain threshold, lambda functions can be triggered to scale resources up or down dynamically, ensuring optimal performance and cost efficiency. Figure 3.1 shows an AWS CloudWatch dashboard.
- **Azure Automation:** Azure Automation provides a cloud-based automation service that allows organizations to create, deploy, and manage runbooks to automate repetitive tasks and processes. By defining workflows and schedules, organizations can automate incident detection and recovery procedures, reducing manual intervention and minimizing downtime.
- **Google Cloud Functions:** Google Cloud Functions enable organizations to build serverless applications that automatically respond to events in GCP. By integrating Cloud Functions with monitoring and alerting services such as Google Cloud Operations Suite monitoring, organizations can trigger automated recovery actions based on predefined conditions, such as scaling resources or restarting failed instances.

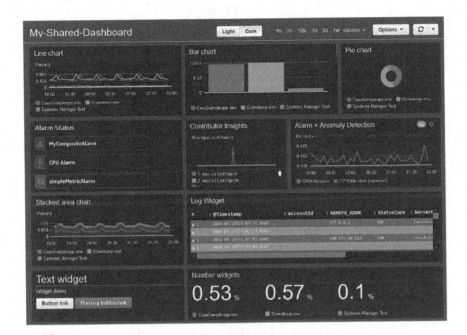

Figure 3.1
AWS CloudWatch dashboard (source: https://aws.amazon.com/blogs/mt/communicate-monitoring-information-by-sharing-amazon-cloudwatch-dashboards/; © 2024, Amazon Web Services, Inc.)

- **Azure Logic Apps:** Azure Logic Apps allow organizations to automate workflows and integrate disparate systems and services across Azure and other platforms. By creating logic workflows with triggers and actions, organizations can automate incident response and recovery processes, orchestrating tasks such as resource scaling, data replication, and failover to ensure continuous operation.

- **Google Cloud Operations Suite (formerly Stackdriver):** Google Cloud Operations Suite provides monitoring, logging, and diagnostics tools that enable organizations to detect and respond to incidents in real time. By setting up alerting policies based on performance metrics and logs, organizations can trigger automated recovery actions using Cloud Functions or other GCP services to mitigate disruptions and maintain service availability.

- **Azure Autoscale:** Azure Autoscale enables organizations to automatically adjust the number of virtual machine (VM) instances or App Service instances based on predefined scaling rules. By monitoring performance metrics such as CPU utilization or request latency, Azure Autoscale can dynamically scale resources to meet changing demand, ensuring optimal performance and availability.

Automation mechanisms can include self-healing mechanisms that identify and resolve issues without human intervention. Following are some examples.

- **AWS EC2 Auto Recovery:** AWS EC2 Auto Recovery automatically detects and recovers failed Elastic Compute Cloud (EC2) instances, minimizing downtime and maintaining application availability. By defining health checks and recovery actions, organizations can enable self-healing capabilities that automatically restart failed instances or replace them with healthy instances to ensure continuous operation.
- **Azure Virtual Machine Scale Sets:** Azure Virtual Machine Scale Sets allow organizations to define scaling policies based on performance metrics or schedule, automatically adjusting the number of VM instances in response to changes in demand. By leveraging auto-scaling capabilities, organizations can ensure high availability and responsiveness without manual intervention.
- **Google Cloud Kubernetes Engine (GKE):** GKE provides built-in auto-scaling and auto-repair features that automatically adjust the number of Kubernetes Pods based on resource utilization and health checks. GKE can automatically restart or replace unhealthy Pods, ensuring application reliability and availability without manual intervention.

CRE teams continuously refine and optimize their automated recovery processes through post-incident analysis and learning. By identifying root causes and bottlenecks in the recovery workflow, they can make data-driven improvements to enhance the speed and effectiveness of automated recovery mechanisms. Ultimately, the goal of automating recovery is to minimize downtime, reduce the impact on customers, and align with Lean principles of efficiency and continuous improvement.

Step 4: Implement Redundancy

This step involves designing systems with redundancy and failover mechanisms to maintain service availability. Redundancy is a critical element of resilience and can significantly reduce the impact of incidents and failures. Organizations implement redundancy by duplicating critical components, resources, or services within their infrastructure. For example, they might use AWS Auto Scaling to maintain duplicate instances of their applications across multiple AZs to ensure that if one AZ experiences issues, traffic can be seamlessly rerouted to a healthy one. This approach minimizes downtime and provides a higher level of service availability.

Additionally, organizations might use AWS services such as Amazon RDS Multi-AZ or DynamoDB Global Tables to replicate databases across different locations, ensuring data consistency and availability even in the face of regional outages.

Other cloud providers offer the following services.

- **Azure Availability Zones:** Azure Availability Zones provide redundant data centers within a region, allowing organizations to distribute their applications and data across multiple physical locations for high availability and fault tolerance. By deploying resources such as VMs, databases, and storage across different AZs, organizations can ensure continuous operation even if one zone experiences issues.
- **Google Cloud Regions and Zones:** Google Cloud offers a global network of data centers organized into regions and zones, allowing organizations to deploy redundant resources in geographically separate locations. By replicating critical services and data across multiple regions and zones, organizations can withstand regional failures and maintain service availability for users worldwide.

- **Azure Traffic Manager:** Azure Traffic Manager enables organizations to distribute incoming traffic across multiple Azure regions or global endpoints, improving application availability and responsiveness. By configuring Traffic Manager with health checks and failover policies, organizations can automatically reroute traffic to healthy endpoints in the event of a region or endpoint failure.

- **Google Cloud Load Balancing:** Google Cloud Load Balancing automatically distributes incoming traffic across multiple instances or regions to ensure high availability and scalability. By configuring load balancers with health checks and failover policies, organizations can achieve redundancy and fault tolerance for their applications, minimizing downtime and improving user experience.

- **Azure SQL Database geo-replication:** Azure SQL Database offers geo-replication capabilities that allow organizations to replicate databases across different Azure regions for disaster recovery and business continuity. By configuring asynchronous replication between primary and secondary databases, organizations can ensure data consistency and availability across geographically dispersed locations.

- **Google Cloud Spanner:** Google Cloud Spanner is a globally distributed, horizontally scalable database service that provides strong consistency and high availability across multiple regions. By replicating data automatically and synchronously across global spans, Spanner ensures data redundancy and fault tolerance, enabling applications to withstand regional outages without data loss or downtime.

- **Azure Blob Storage geo-redundancy:** Azure Blob Storage offers geo-redundant storage (GRS) and zone-redundant storage (ZRS) options for replicating data across multiple Azure regions or zones. By enabling GRS or ZRS replication, organizations can protect their data against regional disasters and ensure data availability and durability for mission-critical applications.

- **Google Cloud Storage regional buckets:** Google Cloud Storage allows organizations to create regional buckets that replicate data across multiple regions within a single geographic area. By storing data redundantly in regional buckets, organizations can achieve high availability and durability, with automatic failover in the event of a regional outage.

By implementing redundancy strategically and testing failover mechanisms continuously, CRE teams can enhance their systems' robustness and resilience, aligning with Lean principles of reducing waste and improving overall efficiency.

Step 5: Test and Validate

This step involves regularly testing recovery procedures to validate their effectiveness and identify areas for improvement. This step also aligns with Lean principles of continuous improvement and eliminating waste, ensuring that recovery processes are efficient and reliable. Testing and validation involve conducting drills, simulations, or exercises to mimic various failure scenarios and evaluate how well the recovery procedures perform. Teams can use tools such as AWS Fault Injection Simulator (FIS), Azure Service Fabric Fault Analysis (SAFA), or Google Cloud Chaos Engineering (GCE) (see more in Chapter 7) to intentionally inject faults and failures into their systems, allowing them to assess how well the systems respond. These tests help identify weaknesses, bottlenecks, or overlooked dependencies in the recovery process, allowing for refinement and optimization.

By regularly testing and validating recovery procedures, CRE teams can build confidence in their ability to respond effectively to incidents. This proactive approach not only reduces downtime and minimizes the impact of failures, but also fosters a culture of continuous learning and improvement within the organization. It ensures that fast recovery practices remain aligned with evolving business needs and technological advancements, ultimately contributing to a more resilient and reliable cloud infrastructure.

Step 6: Prioritize Customer Experience

This step involves prioritizing the restoration of critical user-facing functionalities to maintain a positive customer experience.

This step aligns with Lean principles of delivering value to customers and minimizing disruptions. When incidents occur, ensuring that users can continue to interact with the system smoothly is paramount. During fast recovery, CRE teams prioritize the restoration of essential functionalities that directly impact users. This includes identifying key features, services, or components that are critical for user satisfaction and business continuity. By preserving these user-facing functionalities early in the recovery process, organizations can minimize the impact of downtime and disruptions. This approach aligns with Lean's emphasis on delivering value efficiently and eliminating waste, as it ensures that resources are allocated to the most crucial areas first.

Prioritizing the user experience also involves effective communication with users, keeping them informed about the progress of recovery efforts and setting realistic expectations for service restoration. This not only helps manage user perceptions but also demonstrates transparency and a commitment to customer satisfaction. In essence, this CRE step is about maintaining a positive user experience even in the face of incidents, reinforcing trust and loyalty while swiftly resolving issues.

Step 7: Pursue Continuous Improvement

This step involves analyzing incidents and recovery efforts to continuously enhance the organization's response and recovery capabilities. Lean principles emphasize the ongoing pursuit of efficiency and optimization, and this step aligns perfectly with that philosophy.

After resolving an incident, CRE teams engage in a thorough post-incident analysis. They evaluate the incident's root causes, the effectiveness of the recovery process, and the impact on users and the business. This analysis serves as the foundation for identifying areas of improvement. By adopting a continuous improvement mindset, organizations can iteratively refine their incident response procedures, recovery strategies, and preventive measures. This Lean-inspired approach encourages teams to learn from past incidents, reducing the likelihood of recurrence and enhancing overall system reliability.

Furthermore, continuous improvement extends beyond individual incidents. CRE teams focus on building a culture of learning and adaptation, where every incident becomes an opportunity to refine processes and foster resilience. This iterative approach aligns with Lean's core principle of minimizing waste, as it aims to eliminate sources of inefficiency and enhance the organization's ability to respond to and recover from future challenges effectively. Ultimately, the goal is to create a proactive and resilient environment where incidents are not just resolved but also serve as catalysts for ongoing improvement.

In CRE, incident response and fast recovery are integral components of maintaining high availability and reliability in cloud-based environments. By efficiently addressing incidents and swiftly recovering from disruptions, organizations can minimize the impact on their customers, maintain service quality, and uphold their commitment to reliability and resilience.

Incident Handling

Let us now address the process of incident handling. In CRE, handling incidents is a well-structured and automated process aimed at minimizing time to detect (TTD) and time to recover (TTR) to ensure rapid response and resolution. The CRE approach follows several key principles to achieve this.

- **Proactive monitoring and alerting:** CRE teams implement comprehensive monitoring solutions that continuously track the performance and health of systems and applications. These systems are configured to generate real-time alerts based on predefined thresholds or anomalies. Automation plays a vital role in this phase by enabling the automatic collection of metrics, log analysis, and triggering alerts when deviations occur. This proactive monitoring ensures that issues are detected as soon as they arise, reducing TTD. We will discuss monitoring and alerting in more detail in Chapter 5, "Leveraging Observability, Monitoring, Reliability Metrics, and GenAI: How to Gain Insights, Set Effective Monitoring, Set Service Level Objectives, and Establish Thresholds."

- **Automated incident triage:** Upon receiving alerts, CRE leverages automation to triage incidents swiftly and accurately. Automated incident management tools categorize and prioritize incidents based on severity and potential impact on users and the business. By automating this initial assessment, CRE teams can quickly focus their efforts on high-priority incidents, thus reducing TTD and ensuring faster response times.

- **Runbooks and playbooks:** CRE maintains a library of incident response runbooks and playbooks, which contain predefined procedures for addressing common incidents. These documents include step-by-step instructions, scripts, and commands that guide engineers through the resolution process. Automation is integrated into these runbooks to execute routine tasks automatically. This approach streamlines the incident resolution process, reduces the need for manual intervention, and accelerates TTR.

- **Automated remediation:** CRE embraces the concept of automated remediation, where predefined scripts and workflows are executed automatically to resolve known issues. Automation, such as AWS lambda functions, step functions, automated runbooks, auto failover, auto rollbacks, or similar services, are employed to remediate common problems without human intervention. Automating the recovery process significantly reduces TTR, as the system can heal itself quickly and efficiently.

- **Post-incident analysis and improvement:** Following incident resolution, CRE teams conduct post-incident reviews to analyze the root causes, response effectiveness, and potential areas for improvement. Automation is leveraged to gather and analyze incident data, providing valuable insights for refining incident response procedures, enhancing monitoring thresholds, and preventing recurrence. This continuous improvement cycle ensures that CRE practices become more efficient over time, further reducing TTD and TTR.

Summary

CRE combines proactive monitoring, automated incident handling, and continuous improvement to create a highly efficient incident management process. By leveraging automation at every stage, organizations can significantly reduce TTD and TTR, ensuring minimal disruption to users and maintaining high system reliability.

Q&A

Q: Can you define time to detect and time to recover in greater detail?

Time to detect (TTD) is a critical metric in the field of incident management and CRE. It represents the amount of time it takes to identify and become aware of an incident or issue within a system or application from the moment it first occurs. TTD measures the speed and efficiency with which an organization can detect anomalies, deviations, or problems that might impact the performance, availability, or security of its digital services.

A shorter TTD is desirable in CRE and incident response because it enables organizations to respond rapidly to emerging issues, minimizing the potential impact on users and the business. Achieving a low TTD involves implementing proactive monitoring, alerting systems, and automation to quickly identify and acknowledge incidents as they happen. It allows organizations to initiate the incident response process promptly, investigate the root causes, and take corrective actions to restore normal operations. Reducing TTD is crucial for maintaining high service reliability and minimizing disruptions in the digital age, where swift detection and response to incidents is essential.

Time to recover (TTR) is a crucial metric in the context of incident management and CRE. It represents the amount of time required to fully restore a system, service, or application to its normal operational state after an incident or disruption has occurred. TTR measures the speed and efficiency with which an organization can recover from an incident, minimizing downtime and the associated impact on users and business operations.

A shorter TTR is highly desirable because it means that an organization can respond swiftly and effectively to incidents, reducing the duration of service interruptions and disruptions. Achieving a low TTR involves implementing well-defined incident response procedures, automation, and recovery mechanisms to expedite the restoration of affected systems or services. It also requires thorough post-incident analysis to identify root causes and preventive measures, thereby enhancing the organization's ability to recover rapidly from similar incidents in the future. Minimizing TTR is crucial for maintaining high service reliability, meeting service level agreements (SLAs), meeting service level objectives (SLOs), and ensuring a positive user experience.

Q: What are some of the incident management tools and processes?

For effective incident and case management within the CRE framework, organizations typically require a combination of tools and processes. These tools often include playbooks and incident management systems. Here's a breakdown of the seven key components.

1. **Incident tracking and case management system**
   - **Incident case management system:** An incident tracking and case management system is a centralized platform that allows organizations to log, track, and manage incidents, including their lifecycle, from detection to resolution. These systems provide a structured way to handle incidents, assign ownership, set priorities, and document actions taken.
   - **Ticketing systems:** Many organizations use ticketing systems (e.g., Jira, ServiceNow) as part of their case management approach. These systems help in tracking incidents, assigning tasks to appropriate personnel, and maintaining a record of actions and resolutions.

2. **Playbooks and runbooks**
   - **Incident playbooks:** Incident playbooks are documented, step-by-step guides that outline the response procedures for common incidents. They include predefined actions, decision trees, and escalation paths. Playbooks help response teams follow consistent and efficient processes during incidents.
   - **Runbooks:** Runbooks are similar to playbooks, but may be broader in scope, covering not only incident response but also routine maintenance, troubleshooting, and other operational tasks. They can include automation scripts and procedures for rapid execution. Mature organizations not only have runbooks, but also have invested in tooling to automatically execute those scripts and plug-ins in a timely fashion.

3. **Automation and orchestration tools:** Tools such as AWS Step Functions, AWS AppConfig, Azure Logic Apps, Google Cloud Composer, and third-party orchestration platforms allow organizations to automate workflows and configuration responses during incidents. These tools can execute predefined actions, trigger alerts, and coordinate incident resolution efforts.

4. **Communication and collaboration tools:** Effective communication is crucial during incidents. Collaboration tools such as Slack, Microsoft Teams, and dedicated incident communication platforms help teams communicate in real time, share updates, and collaborate on incident resolution.

5. **Monitoring and alerting tools:** Tools such as AWS Cloud-Watch, Azure Monitor, Google Cloud Operations Suite (formerly Stackdriver), Prometheus, New Relic, Splunk, and Nagios are essential for detecting incidents in real time. They generate alerts based on predefined thresholds and send them to incident response teams and application teams for immediate action.

6. **Knowledge base and documentation:** A knowledge base or documentation repository stores information about past incidents, their resolutions, and lessons learned. It helps incident responders access relevant information quickly and make informed decisions.

7. **Continuous improvement and post-incident analysis:** Tools and platforms for post-incident analysis, such as AWS X-Ray, AWS CloudTrail, Azure Monitor Logs, and Google Cloud Logging, allow organizations to review incident data, identify root causes, and implement preventive measures.

In a CRE environment, organizations aim to streamline incident management processes, minimize downtime, and continuously improve their incident response capabilities. The combination of case management systems, playbooks, automation, and collaboration tools facilitates efficient incident resolution while enabling organizations to learn from incidents and enhance their reliability practices.

Q: What are some of the critical playbooks to keep in mind?

In CRE, it is essential to ensure rapid recovery and have a consistent documented response to incidents. This is usually accomplished by providing standard playbooks and training employees in the processes documented. Besides a consistent and standardized approach to incident response, playbooks are essential for incident response and fast recovery because they provide faster response time, enabling support teams to respond to incidents more quickly and efficiently. Teams do not need to waste time figuring out what to do or who should do specific actions. Instead, they can immediately start implementing documented steps to mitigate the incident's impact and start the recovery process. Playbooks preserve institutional knowledge and incorporate lessons learned from past incidents. Playbooks can be created based on domain areas, such as incident triage, network issues, third-party providers, regional isolation, failover, and core infrastructure service failure.

As an example, a high-quality incident triage playbook contains a set of questions that a tech support team needs to ask while in the middle of an incident. These questions can be categorized into the following primary areas.

1. **Identify the scope of the incident.**
   a. What happened? (What are the symptoms? Indicators? Observations?)
   b. Are there any alarms or alerts triggered on monitoring tools, such as AWS CloudWatch, Azure Monitor, or Google Cloud Monitoring?
   c. Is there a potential trigger (e.g., recent deployment, configuration change)?
   d. What is the scope (e.g., does it affect specific services, components, or geographies)?
   e. What is the nature of the incident (e.g., systems are down, security breach, inability to access [partial or complete])?
2. **Identify the impact.**
   a. How critical is the incident (e.g., complete loss of service, specific function impacted, business critical)?
   b. How many users/customers/systems are impacted?
   c. What is the severity level of the incident? (There should be a well-defined scale and criteria for each parameter or customer experience.)

3. **Conduct a root cause analysis.**
    a. Has your cloud provider reported any service disruptions or outages in the impacted region? Are there any other incidents reported by your cloud provider?
    b. Are there any dependencies on other services (cloud provider or third party)? Have there been any reported issues related to any of those?
    c. Have there been any changes in key metrics before or during the incident?
    d. Have relevant logs been analyzed for error messages? Are there patterns or abnormalities in these logs?
    e. Is there any evidence of resource issues (e.g., CPU, storage, RAM) on cloud instances?
    f. Have there been any recent configuration changes?
    g. What else? Any other reasons you can think of? (Always ask this open question, which is very important because it gives an opportunity to think of any root causes that may have been missed otherwise.)
4. **Conduct next steps.**
    a. What is the process for resolving this type of incident? (This should be well documented in the relevant section of the playbook.)
    b. Has the incident response team been notified? (This includes the right team based on the nature and severity of the incident, including relevant stakeholders and leaders.)
    c. What is the communication plan to inform customers or internal users about the incident?
    d. What is the plan for restoring data or services from backup if needed?
    e. What are the next steps and who is responsible for those? (The playbook needs to provide specific instructions, including roles, names, contact information, who initiates the war room if needed, frequency of updates, any communication channels that need to be open [e.g., Slack or Chime chat], and communications to management and users about the progress and the eventual resolution, as well as the lessons learned and steps taken to prevent this in the future.)

See Appendix A for an Incident Response Checklist Template.

If a company's playbook covers these topics with a sufficient level of detail clearly and concisely and trains proper employees to follow these standards, the tech support team and relevant stakeholders can efficiently and effectively respond to incidents, focusing on the most critical questions to gather essential information, identify the root cause, and work toward resolving the incident promptly.

Chapter 4

Operational Excellence and Change Management

How to Establish Efficient Processes and Maintain Best-in-Class CRE Practices

In this chapter, we will define what operational excellence is and the specific goals associated with it. The goal of operational excellence is to balance how companies get new features into customers' hands safely and implement bug fixes quickly and reliably. Organizations that invest in operational excellence consistently delight customers while building new features, making changes, and dealing with failures.

Operational excellence includes processes (such as metric reporting, incident postmortems, and change management), people (engineers and engineering leaders), and tools (playbooks, monitoring and altering tools, etc.) required to maintain resilient cloud operations (see Figure 4.1).

Operational excellence in cloud reliability engineering (CRE) focuses on efficiently managing cloud resources and services to ensure the reliability, availability, and performance of applications hosted in the cloud. The goal is to maintain a high level of customer satisfaction while handling changes and failures effectively.

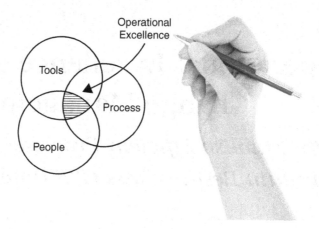

Key Performance Indicators

Engineering leaders must understand that recovering quickly is critical to success. This is where it is crucial to define and measure the health of operations activities. Time to restore (TTR) and time to detect (TTD), introduced in Chapter 3, are some of the key performance indicators (KPIs) offering customers a "business as usual" experience (i.e., customers are not experiencing any issues). Additional operational metrics include the number of customers impacted, number of incidents by severity, number of incidents per app category (critical, noncritical, critical dependency), root cause themes, and number of incidents caused by third-party providers.

Root Cause Analysis

The **root cause analysis** (RCA) is a crucial phase in fostering a culture of continuous improvement within CRE. Teams conduct post-incident reviews to identify root causes and contributing factors behind incidents, enabling the development of preventive measures and the refinement of incident response processes.

Cloud reliability in operational excellence is crucial for organizations relying on cloud services to deliver their applications and services. Quickly identifying root causes and addressing issues helps maintain customer trust, reduces downtime, and ensures a positive user experience, all while optimizing operational costs.

To identify root causes, we recommend using the Lean **"five whys" technique**. This technique involves asking "why" multiple times (five times is considered sufficient in most cases) to drill down to the root cause of a specific problem. Repeatedly asking "why" helps uncover deeper, often overlooked factors contributing to the issue. The goal is to identify the root cause rather than just addressing superficial symptoms or assigning blame for the issue. It starts with identifying the problem, such as the low resilience of a specific system, low availability of your key resource, or vulnerability you uncovered using chaos engineering.

Let's review an example of using the "five whys" technique to identify the root cause of low cloud application resilience.

Problem Statement: The cloud application experiences frequent downtime and outages, resulting in low resilience and an unsatisfactory user experience.

- **Why #1:** Why does the cloud application experience frequent downtime and outages?

  Answer: Because the application's server instances occasionally fail due to server instance (host) issues related to capacity.
- **Why #2:** Why do the server instances occasionally fail and run out of capacity?

  Answer: Because our current application design does not have redundant hosts in place for the server instances.
- **Why #3:** Why doesn't the design and/or cloud provider have redundant hosts for the server instances?

  Answer: Because our organization opted for the least expensive cloud service tier, which doesn't include host redundancy.

- **Why #4:** Why did the organization opt for the least expensive cloud service tier without redundancy?

    Answer: Because the organization's budget constraints led us to choose the most cost-effective option.
- **Why #5:** Why were budget constraints a concern?

    Answer: Because our organization did not allocate sufficient funds for the cloud infrastructure, prioritizing cost savings over improved resilience.

Based on this analysis, we were able to identify the root cause of the low cloud application resilience. The root cause is the lack of capacity in the application infrastructure, which was the organization's decision to prioritize cost savings over improved resilience, leading it to opt for the least expensive cloud service tier or design, which lacks redundancy. As a result, the application experiences frequent downtime and outages whenever server instances fail due to capacity issues, without any backup to maintain availability.

With this root cause identified, your organization can now work on developing a solution. This could involve upgrading to a higher tier with redundant hosts or exploring other ways to enhance resilience within your budget constraints. By addressing the root cause, you can now improve the application's resilience and overall user experience.

Incident Reviews

When things fail, you will want to ensure that your team, as well as your larger engineering community, learns from those failures. You should analyze failures to identify lessons learned and plan improvements. You will want to regularly review your lessons learned with other teams to validate your insights. One technique used is the creation of a blameless incident review, which is common in companies such as Netflix, Amazon, and Capital One, where the goal is to broadly share the learnings, passing the insights on to the engineering community to prevent future incidents.

A **blameless incident review**, or a **blameless postmortem**, as some companies refer to it, is a collaborative process that brings teams together to analyze incidents without assigning blame. Instead of focusing on individual errors, blameless postmortems aim to identify systemic issues and opportunities for improvement, fostering a culture of learning and continuous improvement. During a blameless postmortem, teams delve into the incident to understand what happened, why it happened, how the team responded, and what can be done to prevent similar incidents in the future. The emphasis is on objective analysis and constructive feedback, rather than finger-pointing or punishment.

Advantages of blameless postmortems include the following, from Atlassian's *Incident Management Handbook for Jira Service Management*.

- **Healthy team culture:** By removing the fear of blame, blameless postmortems promote open communication, empathy, and collaboration among team members.
- **Increased incident reporting:** Without the fear of consequences, employees are more likely to report incidents promptly, allowing teams to address issues proactively.
- **Continuous learning:** Blameless postmortems encourage teams to discuss mistakes openly, share ideas for improvement, and embrace a culture of learning and adaptation.
- **Improved support and communication:** Teams can support one another more effectively when blame is removed from the equation, fostering stronger relationships and trust.
- **Empowerment for application teams:** Employees feel empowered to contribute ideas and solutions without fear of retribution, leading to more innovative and effective problem-solving.

Blameless culture originated in the healthcare and avionics industries, where mistakes can be fatal. These industries nurture an environment where every "mistake" is seen as an opportunity to strengthen the system. When postmortems shift from allocating blame to investigating the systematic reasons why an individual or team had incomplete or incorrect information, effective prevention plans can be put in place. You can fix systems and processes to better support people making the right choices when designing and maintaining complex systems.

The best practices for implementing blameless postmortems include the following.

- **Communicate openness:** Ensure that teams understand that blameless postmortems are about learning and improvement, not punishment.
- **Encourage honesty:** Foster a culture of honesty and accountability, where employees feel comfortable admitting mistakes and sharing their experiences.
- **Build a timeline:** Establish a clear timeline of the incident to ensure that all stakeholders have a shared understanding of what occurred.
- **Consistency is key:** Ensure that all postmortems follow a blameless approach to maintain trust and credibility within the organization.
- **Gain leadership support:** Obtain buy-in from company leaders to support the transition to a blameless culture and allocate resources for training and implementation.
- **Collaborate across teams:** Invite representatives from various teams to participate in postmortems to gain diverse perspectives and identify potential improvements.
- **Make data-driven decisions:** Use the insights gathered from blameless postmortems to make informed decisions about process improvements and preventive measures.
- **Review and approval:** Assign responsibility for reviewing postmortem findings and approving recommended actions to ensure accountability and follow-through.

Amazon uses a mechanism called the **Correction of Error (COE) process** for blame-free post-incident analysis. This lets engineers analyze a system after an incident to avoid recurrences in the future. These incidents also help teams learn more about how their systems and processes work. That knowledge often leads to actions that help other incident scenarios, not just the prevention of a specific recurrence. Although post-event analysis is part of the COE process, it is different from a postmortem, because the focus is on corrective actions, not just documenting failures.

The COE process consists of a post-event analysis. It is imperative that the negative impact caused by the event be mitigated before the COE process begins. This lets you do the following.

- Dive deep into the sequence of events leading up to the incident.
- Find the root cause of the problem and identify remediation actions.
- Analyze the impact of the incident on the business and its customers.
- Identify and track action items that prevent problem recurrences.

It is important to remember that COE is not a mechanism designed to assign blame for problems. Instead, its primary goal is to enhance visibility into areas requiring improvement. Cultivating an environment that encourages individuals to bring forth issues fosters increased awareness of areas needing attention. Human behavior tends to repeat actions that are positively reinforced while avoiding those that incur penalties.

Most importantly, a COE is not a tool for punishing employees following a negative event. Rather, its purpose is to ensure ongoing enhancement throughout an application's lifecycle. Frequently, those most knowledgeable about an incident have the greatest stake in its outcome. By incentivizing comprehensive disclosure of events, we cultivate a culture that rewards transparency and empowers individuals closest to the issue to contribute to solutions rather than being viewed as part of the problem.

COE includes identifying the following.

- What happened?
- What was the impact on customers and your business?
- What was the root cause?
- What data do you have to support this (especially metrics and graphs)?

- What were the critical pillar implications, especially cost and security? When architecting workloads, you make trade-offs between pillars based upon your business context. These business decisions can drive your engineering priorities. You might optimize to reduce cost at the expense of reliability in development environments, or, for mission-critical solutions, you might optimize reliability with increased costs. Security is always job zero, as you have to protect your customers.
- What lessons did you learn?
- What corrective actions are you taking (include task, owner, and completion date)?
- What are some related items (e.g., trouble tickets)?

Appendix B describes COE structure and components in more detail.

Once drafted, COEs are reviewed by the immediate team, as well as other teams. At Amazon, there is a group of COE Bar Raisers who raise the bar on COE quality. As explained in a post on the Amazon Web Services (AWS) Cloud Operations blog, an engineer can apply to become a COE through a learning and mentoring process. High-impact COEs are usually reviewed during operational meetings.

MS Azure follows a similar process and provides detailed post-mortems internally as well as externally.[1]

Google also has a postmortem culture, as discussed in *Site Reliability Engineering*. The primary goals of writing a postmortem are to ensure that the incident is documented, that all contributing root cause(s) are well understood, and, especially, that effective preventive actions are put in place to reduce the likelihood and/or impact of recurrence. Google teams use a variety of techniques for RCA and choose the technique best suited to their services. Postmortems are expected after any significant undesirable event. Writing a postmortem is not punishment—it is a learning opportunity for the entire company. The postmortem process does present an inherent cost in

---

1 For Microsoft postmortem examples, see https://devblogs.microsoft.com/devopsservice/?p=17665 and https://status.dev.azure.com/_event/116182577/postmortem.

terms of time or effort, so application leaders and teams are deliberate in choosing when to write one. Teams have some internal flexibility, but common postmortem triggers include the following:

- User-visible downtime or degradation beyond a certain threshold
- Data loss of any kind
- On-call engineer intervention (release rollback, rerouting of traffic, etc.)
- A resolution time above some threshold
- A monitoring failure (which usually implies manual incident discovery)

It is important to define postmortem criteria before an incident occurs so that everyone knows when a postmortem is necessary. In addition to these objective triggers, any stakeholder may request a postmortem for an event.

Postmortems are part of your company's continuous improvement culture. Every operational incident should be treated as an opportunity to improve the operations of your systems and share learnings across your organization. By understanding the needs of your customers and services; predefining runbooks for routine activities; using playbooks to guide incident resolution, scripts for operations as code, runbook automation tooling, and chaos testing scenarios; and offering situational awareness, your reliability teams or, in the case of Google, the app teams following the "You build it, you own it" (YBYO) approach, will be better prepared to respond effectively when incidents occur.

Change Management

Change management in CRE refers to the structured processes and practices used to manage and control incident-related task "changes" to a cloud-based system, infrastructure, or service. This practice is critical for maintaining the reliability, availability, and performance of cloud services. Change management ensures that the application causing the incident is fixed, but also that all other applications that can benefit from the change implement the change. This technique raises the engineering levels across the organization, rather than only at the application that caused the incident.

Almost 70% of incidents are caused by changes. Changes to your workload or its environment must be anticipated and accommodated to achieve reliable operation of the workload, system, or component that is experiencing the change. Changes include those externally imposed on your workload, such as spikes in demand, as well as those from within the organization, such as feature deployments and security patches. To establish efficient processes and maintain CRE practices, a company needs to focus on multiple aspects of successful change management. Table 4.1 outlines the components of CRE change management.

Table 4.1
CRE Change Management Components

Component	Description	Example
Change management policies	Establish clear policies outlining procedures for initiating, reviewing, and approving changes to cloud-based systems. Define roles, responsibilities, escalation paths, and evaluation criteria.	AWS provides documentation on creating change management policies using AWS Service Catalog and AWS Organizations.
Approval workflow	Implement an approval workflow for reviewing and approving changes by relevant stakeholders. Document approvals and track change request progress.	Azure DevOps allows custom approval processes for infrastructure as code (IaC) template changes.
Risk assessment	Conduct risk assessments to evaluate the potential impacts of proposed changes on reliability, availability, and performance. Identify and mitigate risks before implementation.	Google Cloud's Risk Management Framework offers guidelines for assessing and managing risks in cloud infrastructure changes.
Change management documentation	Maintain comprehensive documentation of all changes, including requests, approvals, implementation details, and outcomes. Ensure accessibility and real-time updates for transparency and accountability.	AWS Systems Manager's Change Manager feature enables documenting and tracking changes to AWS resources.

(Continued)

Component	Description	Example
Testing and validation	Perform thorough testing and validation of changes in controlled environments before deployment. Validate against predefined criteria for performance, security, and reliability standards.	Azure DevOps pipelines facilitate automated testing and validation of infrastructure changes using Azure Test Plans.
Scheduling	Develop schedules for implementing changes to minimize operational disruptions and maximize availability. Coordinate deployments with maintenance windows and peak usage periods to minimize user impact.	Google Cloud Scheduler automates scheduling of changes and maintenance tasks across Google Cloud services.
Monitoring and alerting	Implement monitoring and alerting systems to detect and respond to issues resulting from changes. Monitor key metrics and set up alerts to notify relevant teams of deviations from expected behavior.	AWS CloudWatch offers monitoring and alerting capabilities to track performance metrics and trigger alarms based on predefined thresholds.
Communication and training	Communicate change plans, progress, and outcomes to stakeholders and affected teams for transparency and alignment. Provide training and documentation to help teams adapt to changes effectively.	Microsoft Learn provides training resources and tutorials on Azure DevOps for implementing change management practices.
Post-implementation review	Conduct reviews to evaluate change effectiveness and identify improvement opportunities. Gather feedback from stakeholders and teams involved in the process to inform future iterations.	Google Cloud's Incident Response and Postmortem process includes post-incident reviews to assess the impact of change on system reliability.
Audit and compliance	Ensure compliance with regulatory requirements and internal policies by documenting and auditing change management processes. Maintain records for auditing purposes.	AWS Config offers continuous monitoring and compliance checks to ensure that changes comply with security and compliance standards.
Change Management Checklist*	Include a detailed checklist covering steps and requirements for effective change management. Cover each component, from policy development to post-implementation review.	The Change Management Checklist by the Cloud Native Computing Foundation (CNCF) provides a guide for implementing change management best practices in cloud-native environments.

*See Appendix C for the detailed checklist.

By implementing these components of change management in CRE, organizations can effectively manage and control changes to cloud-based systems, ensuring reliability, availability, and performance while minimizing risks and disruptions.

Each of these components is crucial for your change management process and has to be part of your documented process. Removing one of these components can lead to incidents and operational failures.

Case Study

Let's review a hypothetical example of a company operating an e-commerce platform on Google Cloud experiencing intermittent performance issues during peak traffic periods. After conducting an RCA, it is determined that the current configuration of its Compute Engine instances is not optimized to handle sudden spikes in user traffic.

Consider the following change management process.

- **Change management policies**
  - The company establishes clear policies outlining procedures for initiating, reviewing, and approving changes to its Google Cloud infrastructure.
  - Roles and responsibilities are defined, with designated personnel responsible for overseeing Compute Engine configuration changes. For instance, the Cloud Operations team is responsible for overseeing Compute Engine configuration changes, which includes reviewing proposed changes, assessing their impact, and ensuring compliance with established policies and procedures. Additionally, the team works closely with system administrators and developers to coordinate and implement these changes seamlessly while minimizing any potential disruptions to the cloud infrastructure.

- **Approval workflow**
  - An approval workflow is implemented to ensure that proposed changes to the Compute Engine configuration undergo thorough review by the infrastructure team and DevOps engineers.
  - Changes are documented and tracked using Google Cloud's Deployment Manager, ensuring transparency and accountability throughout the approval process.
- **Risk assessment**
  - A risk assessment is conducted to evaluate the potential impact of the proposed Compute Engine configuration changes on the reliability and availability of the e-commerce platform.
  - Mitigation strategies are identified to address any potential risks, such as instance downtime or performance degradation.
- **Change management documentation**
  - Comprehensive documentation is maintained for all proposed changes to the Compute Engine configuration, including change requests, approvals, and implementation details.
  - Documentation is updated in real time using Google Cloud's Cloud Source Repositories, providing visibility into the change management process.
- **Testing and validation**
  - The proposed Compute Engine configuration changes are thoroughly tested in a controlled environment before deployment to production.
  - Automated testing scripts are utilized to validate the changes against predefined performance and reliability criteria, ensuring that they meet the required standards.
- **Scheduling**
  - A schedule is developed for implementing the Compute Engine configuration changes during off-peak hours to minimize disruption to the e-commerce platform's operations.
  - Coordination with the marketing team ensures that the changes are deployed during periods of lower user activity.

- **Monitoring and alerting**
  - Monitoring and alerting systems are implemented to detect any unexpected behavior or performance issues following the deployment of the Compute Engine configuration changes.
  - Key performance metrics, such as instance CPU utilization and network throughput, are continuously tracked using Google Cloud Monitoring. Alerts are configured to promptly notify the appropriate teams whenever there is any deviation from expected performance, allowing for quick responses to potential issues. This monitoring tool integrates with the broader Google Cloud operations suite, offering a comprehensive approach to maintaining optimal system health and performance.
- **Communication and training**
  - Change plans, progress, and outcomes are communicated to stakeholders and affected teams to ensure transparency and alignment.
  - Training sessions are conducted to familiarize team members with the updated Compute Engine configuration and any operational changes resulting from the deployment.
- **Post-implementation review**
  - A post-implementation review is conducted to evaluate the effectiveness of the Compute Engine configuration changes and identify any areas for improvement.
  - Feedback from stakeholders and teams involved in the change management process is gathered to inform future iterations and optimize the process further.
- **Audit and compliance**
  - Documentation of the Compute Engine configuration changes and associated change management processes is maintained for auditing purposes.
  - Google Cloud's Audit Logs are used to ensure continuous monitoring and compliance with security and regulatory requirements throughout the change management lifecycle.

- **Change outcome:** Following the implementation of the optimized Compute Engine configuration, the e-commerce platform experiences improved performance and reliability during peak traffic periods. User satisfaction increases, and the company's reputation for providing a reliable online shopping experience is enhanced. Additionally, the structured change management process ensures that similar performance issues are proactively addressed in the future, contributing to the overall reliability and availability of the cloud-based service on Google Cloud.

Heraclitus, the Greek philosopher, is known to have said, "Change is the only constant in life." The same applies to cloud engineering. The company that does not manage its changes well is bound to fail.

Architecture and Reliability Assessments

To assess your infrastructure against best practices and enable optimization, your organization has the ability to establish architecture standards (with different requirements based on the criticality of the application), operational readiness reviews (ORRs) for those applications with high-severity incidents impacting customers in production, and launch readiness reviews (LRRs) for those brand-new applications just ready to hit production.

AWS also offers the AWS Well-Architected Tool. This tool is a valuable resource for organizations seeking to ensure that their cloud infrastructure adheres to best practices and is optimized for performance, security, and reliability. This tool provides a systematic framework for evaluating the architectural design of your AWS workloads across various dimensions, including operational excellence, security, reliability, performance efficiency, and cost optimization.

By conducting these assessments, organizations gain insights into areas where their infrastructure can be improved, ensuring that it aligns with AWS's architectural best practices. The tool's recommendations and insights help organizations make informed decisions, identify potential risks, and prioritize enhancements, ultimately leading to the creation of more resilient, efficient, and cost-effective cloud architectures.

The Google Cloud Platform offers various tools and services to conduct architecture assessments for optimization, including the Google Cloud Architecture Framework and Cloud Monitoring. The Google Cloud Architecture Framework provides best practices, reference architectures, and design patterns to help organizations design, deploy, and optimize their cloud environments effectively. It offers guidance on architecture principles, such as scalability, reliability, security, and cost optimization, to ensure that solutions meet business requirements and align with industry standards. Additionally, Cloud Monitoring allows users to monitor the performance, availability, and health of their cloud resources in real time, providing insights into potential bottlenecks, inefficiencies, and areas for improvement. By leveraging these tools, organizations can assess their cloud architectures comprehensively and identify opportunities for optimization to enhance performance, reduce costs, and maximize value from their cloud investments.

Microsoft Azure provides several tools and services for conducting architecture assessments for optimization, including Azure Advisor and the Azure Well-Architected Framework. Azure Advisor offers personalized recommendations and best practices for optimizing Azure resources across various categories, such as performance, security, reliability, and cost. It analyzes resource configurations, usage patterns, and industry benchmarks to identify opportunities for improving efficiency, enhancing security, and reducing expenses. Additionally, the Azure Well-Architected Framework provides a set of guiding principles, design patterns, and assessment tools to help organizations build and operate scalable, resilient, and efficient cloud architectures. It offers guidance on key pillars, such as operational excellence, security, reliability, performance efficiency, and cost optimization, to enable organizations to assess their architectures comprehensively and implement best practices for optimization. By utilizing these tools, organizations can evaluate their cloud architectures effectively and make informed decisions to optimize performance, reduce risks, and drive business value.

Summary

As we have shown in this chapter, operational excellence and change management are fundamental pillars of CRE that play a pivotal role in ensuring the reliability, availability, and performance of cloud-based systems and services. By adopting structured processes, best practices, and effective communication strategies, organizations can enhance their operational capabilities and respond efficiently to incidents and changes in the cloud environment.

Q&A

Q: What are some common ways to measure the effectiveness of a CRE change management process for a company?

Effective change management is integral to maintaining cloud reliability and ensuring that changes, updates, and improvements are carried out in a controlled and reliable manner. It minimizes the risks associated with cloud services, enhances service quality, and builds trust with users and stakeholders. It is important to continuously measure the quality of this process. Following are some metrics to consider.

- **Change success rate:** Measure how many changes are successfully implemented without causing service disruptions.
- **Change failure rate:** Track the number of changes that result in failures or issues requiring rollback.
- **Change lead time:** Calculate the time it takes from the request for a change to its successful implementation.

- **Emergency changes:** Monitor the frequency of emergency or unscheduled changes, as they can indicate underlying reliability issues.
- **Incident rate:** Keep an eye on the number of incidents or outages that can be attributed to recent changes.
- **Customer satisfaction:** Collect feedback from users or customers to gauge their satisfaction with service quality and reliability.

Q: What are the key concepts of operational excellence in CRE?

Operational excellence in CRE may include one or several of the following categories.

- **Reliability:** Cloud-based applications need to be available and perform as expected. Metrics include availability and uptime.
- **Operations:** Companies need to manage and maintain cloud resources. This includes provisioning, scaling, monitoring, and troubleshooting.
- **Excellence:** Companies need to strive for the highest standards of operational performance, efficiency, and quality in cloud management and delivery.
- **Cloud operations:** Companies need to maintain effective operations, minimizing waste and reducing time to discover and resolve incidents.
- **Monitoring and alerting:** Companies need to implement robust monitoring and alerting systems to continuously track the health and performance of cloud resources. When anomalies or issues are detected, alerts are triggered for rapid response.
- **Toil elimination—automation:** Companies must leverage automation tools and scripts to streamline routine operational tasks, such as resource provisioning, scaling, and configuration

management. Automation reduces the risk of manual errors and ensures consistency.

- **Scalability:** Designing cloud-based systems to be scalable, both vertically (adding more resources to a single instance) and horizontally (adding more instances), allows systems to handle varying workloads and traffic.
- **Resilience:** Companies must implement redundancy and failover mechanisms to ensure that services remain available, even in the event of hardware failures or other disruptions. This includes data replication, load balancing, and disaster recovery planning.
- **Security:** Companies need to develop and enforce strong security practices to protect data and applications hosted in the cloud. This includes identity and access management, encryption, and compliance with security standards and regulations.
- **Cost optimization:** Companies must continuously monitor and optimize cloud costs to ensure that resources are used efficiently. This might involve identifying and eliminating under utilized resources and selecting cost-effective pricing models.
- **Change management:** Companies must implement controlled change management processes to ensure that updates, patches, and configuration changes are made without disrupting service availability.
- **Incident response:** Companies must develop and practice incident response plans to address issues and outages promptly. This includes documenting procedures, conducting post-incident reviews, and applying lessons learned to prevent similar incidents in the future.
- **Collaboration:** Companies must foster collaboration and communication among different teams, such as development, operations, and security, to ensure that cloud operations are aligned with business objectives.

Chapter 5

Leveraging Observability, Monitoring, Reliability Metrics, and GenAI

How to Gain Insights, Set Effective Monitoring, Set Service Level Objectives, and Establish Thresholds

Ensuring the availability of cloud services is a major goal for organizations of all sizes and across diverse industries. However, the complexity of modern systems demands robust observability, better monitoring with custom alerting mechanisms, and proactive reliability metrics to validate service level objectives in preparation for failure.

Reliability Engineering Capabilities

Key capabilities in reliability engineering include observability, monitoring, and alerting—all of which play a pivotal role in keeping systems resilient and ensuring quick recovery from failures. By leveraging these capabilities, organizations can effectively manage the complexity of cloud-based systems, maintain optimal performance, and safeguard against disruptions. The following sections will explore these foundational concepts in greater detail, highlighting how observability and cloud monitoring are implemented to ensure system health and business continuity.

Observability

Observability in cloud reliability engineering refers to the capability of correlating data to gain insights into the internal workings of complex cloud-based applications by collecting and analyzing data from various sources. It includes monitoring, tracing, logging, and analyzing data from multiple sources to remediate and prevent issues. If the analysis shows a potential issue, alerting is set up to notify cloud engineers when a threshold is crossed. The cause may include full-service outages, high error rates, latency or availability issues, or performance issues impacting customers.

Cloud Monitoring

Cloud monitoring ensures that the application and infrastructure that are running to serve business needs are operating optimally, tracking and displaying cloud data across different regions, zones, applications, hosts, dependencies, and logs and generating the insights necessary for informed decisions. Dashboards and visualization are the foundation for engineers to conduct investigations, but we know we can't have engineers with eyes on glass 24/7, as that is not cost-effective. Monitoring allows teams to set up alerts and policies, based on service level indicators (SLIs) or targets, and to be notified when those thresholds are breached, which usually indicates something is wrong with the application and that there is a potential impact to customers.

Observability and cloud monitoring form the cornerstone of any cloud reliability strategy. It is critical for companies to establish continuous monitoring on many levels (e.g., based on application criticality, service tier, or line of business) to gain insights into the performance and health of their cloud resources.

Service Level Objectives and Service Level Indicators

A service level objective (SLO) is defined as a target value for a given SLI over a period of time. SLOs give us reliability metrics based on how well cloud-based applications are functioning for our customers. They allow organizations to determine where to invest their engineering capacity to improve services. SLIs can be configured based on factors such as service uptime, latency, availability, and responsiveness.

SLI targets alone will not indicate the aggregation of errors over a period of time. This is why we need to consider the concept of an **error budget**. The error budget provides a clear, objective metric that determines how unreliable the service is allowed to be within the given period, as illustrated in the example in Figure 5.1. In this example, the team has exhausted its error budget in 21 days and needs to prioritize (1) investing in improving resilience and (2) removing technical debt to meet its SLI target in the future.

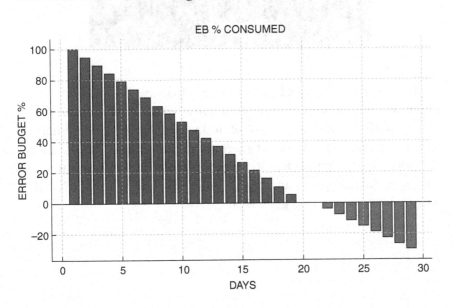

Figure 5.1
Exhausting an error budget

For example, suppose a company has an SLO of 99% availability. The error budget would be 1%, and that 1% in a 28-day window would equate to 6.72 hours of downtime. If the SLI dips below 99% during that window, the application or customer journey has exhausted its error budget and is no longer meeting the SLO. Figure 5.2 shows an example related to stability and user experience based on errors.

Figure 5.2
Mobile app stability
SLI sample

Leveraging SLOs to safeguard the most critical business revenue–generating cloud applications is a great enhancement over traditional alerting with thousands of individual infrastructure metrics (e.g., CPU, disk, input/output operations per second [IOPS], memory utilization). With SLOs, CRE organizations can focus on the most important business-relevant health indicators and react much more quickly when something goes wrong.

Ten-Step Process for Creating Effective Monitoring

There is a standard ten-step process that allows companies to create effective monitoring, choose SLOs, and establish proper thresholds in CRE.

Step 1. Define key metrics: Identify the critical metrics and key performance indicators (KPIs) that matter most to your business, application, or service. This could include availability, response times, error rates, throughput, resource utilization, and any other parameters relevant to your system's reliability and performance.

Step 2. Design and implement monitoring: Choose monitoring tools and implement monitoring mechanisms that can collect the data necessary for your metrics. Cloud platforms often offer built-in monitoring services, and third-party tools are available as well.

Step 3. Define SLOs: Identify the specific, measurable objectives that define the desired level of service quality and reliability.

Step 4. Establish SLIs: Identify the specific metrics or measurements that quantify the quality of service. For example, if response time is a critical metric, the SLI could be "99th percentile response time."

Step 5. Calculate SLI targets: Based on historical data and user expectations, calculate the targets for your SLIs. For example, you might set a 99th percentile response time target at 200 milliseconds.

Step 6. Create error budgets: Identify the allowed margin of error in meeting the SLOs. This is essential for balancing innovation and reliability. For instance, you might set an error budget of 1% for the 99th percentile response time. When this budget is exhausted, you may prioritize reliability over new feature development.

Step 7. Configure alerting and thresholds: Set up alerting rules that are triggered when metrics breach predefined thresholds. Thresholds should be based on your SLOs and error budgets. Alerts should be designed to notify you before you exceed your error budget.

Step 8. Implement distributed tracing: Distributed tracing is a mechanism that helps track application requests as they flow from frontend to backend services. Application teams can use distributed tracing to troubleshoot requests that exhibit some sort of performance issue, such as high latency or high errors. Using end-to-end distributed tracing allows engineers to visualize the full journey of a request—from frontend to backend—and pinpoint any performance failures or bottlenecks that occurred along the way.

Step 9. Cross-functional collaboration: Establish effective communication among development, product, and other relevant teams. This collaboration ensures that SLOs, SLIs, and monitoring strategies align with the broader business and operational goals.

Step 10. Experiment and iterate: Use your error budget to experiment and innovate. Allocate a portion of the budget to introduce new features or improvements while ensuring that your reliability remains within acceptable bounds. Once you have some confidence in the data that has been collected and the policies that have been put in place to follow your SLOs, ensure that your site reliability engineers assign capacity to those applications with SLOs that are in trouble, with the intent to improve their stability and follow best practices. These remediations should be targeted to the SLI that is breaching the target first.

It's important that you regularly review your SLOs, SLIs, and thresholds with leaders, engineers, and the product team. Most engineering-led tech companies have established team-, division-, and enterprise-level operational excellence meetings to review these indicators and other insights about cloud application performance and advancements. Adjust these indicators as necessary based on changing user expectations, business priorities, and specific expected system performance. Remember, not every system or application must be treated the same way. Different experiences require different indicators and targets. Continuously analyze the data to identify trends and areas for improvement.

Maturity Levels

Organizations progress through four maturity levels in their observability, monitoring, and SLO implementation, as illustrated in Figure 5.3 and described in the list that follows.

Level 1—Basic monitoring: At this stage, organizations focus on fundamental metrics such as CPU usage, memory usage, errors, latency, and disk utilization. These metrics provide a foundational understanding of system health but lack granularity.

Level 2—Default SLIs: Organizations establish default SLIs based on historical performance or predefined goals across the company. While this approach offers some standardization, it might not fully align with specific customer needs or critical business processes.

Level 3—Defined customer journeys: At this stage, organizations refine their monitoring strategy by defining specific customer journeys or user experiences. SLIs are tailored to the criticality of each journey, ensuring that resources are allocated based on their impact on business outcomes.

Level 4—Formal SLOs and error budget policies: Organizations implement error budget policies and enforcement mechanisms in collaboration with product teams and leadership. Error budgets serve as a threshold for acceptable service degradation, enabling proactive management of reliability and prioritization of improvements.

Figure 5.3
Four maturity levels

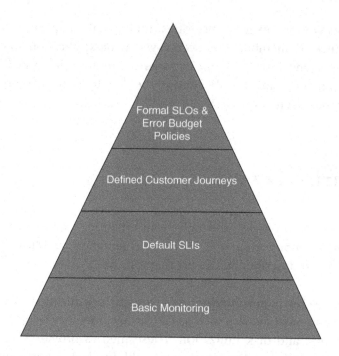

By progressing through these maturity levels, organizations can strengthen their observability practices, refine their monitoring capabilities, and effectively manage SLOs to ensure optimal reliability and performance.

The application of cloud reliability monitoring and alerting varies across industries and company sizes. A robust set of monitoring and alerting tools is available to ensure smooth, incident-free operations. We will explore the available tools in the section that follows.

Monitoring and Alerting Tools

Tools such as AWS CloudWatch, Azure Monitor, Azure Application Insights, the Google Cloud operations suite (formerly Stackdriver) for monitoring and logging, Prometheus, New Relic, Splunk, and Nagios are essential for detecting incidents in real time. They generate alerts based on predefined thresholds and send them to incident response teams for immediate action.

- **AWS CloudWatch:** A comprehensive monitoring service that provides real-time visibility into the operational health of your applications, infrastructure, and services. It collects and tracks metrics, logs, and events, enabling you to monitor resource utilization, set alarms, and gain a holistic view of your Amazon Web Services (AWS) environment.
- **AWS CloudTrail:** Offers a trail of API calls made on your AWS account, providing an audit log that is invaluable for security and compliance monitoring.
- **AWS X-Ray:** A powerful tool for gaining insights into the performance of your applications. It helps you identify bottlenecks and troubleshoot errors in distributed microservices applications by tracing requests as they travel through various AWS services and components. This end-to-end visibility aids in optimizing application performance and ensuring a seamless user experience.
- **AWS Config:** Another essential tool for monitoring and managing the configuration of your AWS resources. It helps you assess, audit, and evaluate your AWS resource configurations for compliance with best practices and policies, allowing you to proactively detect and rectify any configuration drift or non-compliance.
- **AWS Service Health Dashboard:** Provides up-to-date information on the status of AWS services and regions. It's a crucial resource for understanding the operational health of the AWS services you rely on and for staying informed about any ongoing issues or outages.
- **Google Cloud's operations suite:** Includes observability services that help you understand the behavior, health, and performance of your applications.
- **Cloud Monitoring:** Collects metrics, events, and metadata from Google Cloud, AWS, synthetic monitors, and application instrumentation.

- **Google Cloud Trace:** A distributed tracing system for Google Cloud that collects latency data from applications and displays it in near-real time in the Google Cloud console.
- **Azure Monitor:** A combination of three unique services—Azure Monitor, Log Analytics, and Application Insights—that provides powerful end-to-end monitoring of your applications and the components they rely on.

There are a few non-cloud provider-related commercial off-the-shelf (COTS) products that are worth mentioning in this area.

- **New Relic:** New Relic offers powerful insights into your system stack by correlating issues across the entire infrastructure. It provides actionable data to debug and collaborate directly from your IDE, enhancing productivity with artificial intelligence (AI)–driven assistance at each step. This all-in-one connected experience helps teams quickly identify, diagnose, and resolve problems, ensuring system reliability and performance optimization.
- **Splunk:** The Splunk Cloud Platform transforms vast amounts of raw data into clear, actionable insights, enabling organizations to resolve operational issues quickly and enhance system performance. With its powerful data analytics tools, it provides visibility into infrastructure, helping teams proactively manage and optimize operations.
- **Downdetector:** Downdetector provides real-time status and uptime monitoring for over 12,000 services across 45+ countries. It tracks a wide range of services, including telecommunications, online banking, websites, and apps, helping businesses and users quickly identify outages and service disruptions and stay informed about service reliability and performance.
- **Observe:** Observe aggregates data from several tools and offers a multitude of APIs to ingest data and create correlations that allow app teams to solve for incidents more quickly. It also reduces the time to restore and, in many cases due to its power of correlation, generates just-in-time root cause analysis (RCA).

- **Dynatrace:** This solution is a single source of truth for your cloud platforms, allowing you to monitor the health of your entire Azure infrastructure.
- **Jaeger:** Jaeger is a distributed tracing observability platform. Such platforms are essential for modern software applications that are architected as microservices. Jaeger maps the flow of requests and data as they traverse a distributed system. These requests may make calls to multiple services, which might introduce their own delays or errors. Jaeger connects the dots between these disparate components, helping to identify performance bottlenecks, troubleshoot errors, and improve overall application reliability. Jaeger is 100% open source, cloud native, and infinitely scalable.

These monitoring tools collectively empower organizations to maintain the reliability and health of their AWS resources, ensuring optimal performance and minimizing downtime.

Following are key takeaways from known failures.

- **Failures happen:** These incidents demonstrate that even industry giants are susceptible to cloud outages. No system is entirely immune to failures, emphasizing the importance of vigilance and preparedness.
- **Proactive monitoring:** Swift identification of anomalies and proactive monitoring are vital for minimizing downtime. Investing in advanced monitoring tools, anomaly detection, and performance profiling is essential.
- **Robust incident response:** Having an effective incident response plan is crucial. The ability to mobilize teams quickly, communicate transparently, and make data-driven decisions can significantly reduce the impact of outages.
- **Continuous improvement:** Regular post-incident reviews are essential. These should focus on learning from past failures, refining monitoring strategies, and enhancing incident response procedures.

In the rapidly evolving landscape of cloud computing, these types of outages, while still possible, are less likely to happen. The cloud industry has made substantial progress in improving infrastructure, architecture, and monitoring practices. Cloud providers such as AWS, Google, and Microsoft have enhanced their infrastructure to include multiple data centers and geographic regions. This reduces the likelihood of a service-wide outage.

Cloud providers and organizations have adopted more advanced monitoring and alerting systems that can detect anomalies and performance issues in real time, allowing for quicker incident response. There is a greater emphasis on incident response planning, with organizations conducting regular drills to ensure that teams are well prepared to tackle unexpected issues. While these advancements make outages less likely, they don't eliminate the possibility entirely. Emerging technologies, software bugs, human errors, and unforeseen circumstances can still lead to disruption.

Case Study: AI's Impact on CRE

AI advancement has impacted CRE in multiple ways. As defined in Wikipedia, "Generative artificial intelligence (generative AI, GenAI, or GAI) is a subset of artificial intelligence that uses generative models to produce text, images, videos, or other forms of data. These models learn the underlying patterns and structures of their training data and use them to produce new data based on the input, which often comes in the form of natural language prompts."

Microsoft has published a customer story describing how it partnered with AT&T to improve engineering experience with Azure and GenAI. In this case, the goals include the following:

- To enable IT professionals to request resources such as additional virtual machines (VMs) when they are running out of storage or if they are having a computer problem

- To migrate legacy code into modern code, which will help accelerate developers' productivity and let them focus on creating more modern tools and experiences for AT&T customers and employees

This case underscores the critical role of resiliency in ensuring the smooth operation of essential business functions.

The integration of GenAI and automation tools plays a significant role in preventing and mitigating outages. AI-driven systems can identify issues faster than humans can, and take corrective actions. Here are some examples.

- **Anomaly detection:** AI can analyze vast datasets to detect subtle anomalies, which can be early indicators of issues.

    When coupled with advanced monitoring systems, GenAI becomes a real-time guardian of cloud services. For instance, if a sudden performance bottleneck threatens to disrupt a critical application, AI swiftly intervenes. It can allocate additional resources to alleviate the strain or intelligently reroute traffic to avoid service degradation. This dynamic response ensures that disruptions are contained and addressed before they impact end users.

- **Predictive maintenance:** AI can forecast when hardware components or services are likely to fail, allowing for proactive maintenance.

    AI leverages its capacity to analyze historical data comprehensively. Imagine a scenario in which a cloud service is about to confront capacity limitations during an unexpected traffic surge. Through its analytical prowess, AI can foresee this impending challenge. Consequently, it prompts the system to proactively adjust its resources, such as spinning up additional servers and thereby ensuring a seamless user experience. This predictive ability minimizes the risk of service interruptions due to unforeseen surges.

- **Dynamic resource scaling:** AI-driven auto-scaling solutions can automatically adjust resources based on traffic patterns, preventing performance degradation.

  AI systems excel at understanding workload patterns and resource utilization. For instance, consider a cloud application that experiences varying levels of user activity throughout the day. AI continually assesses these patterns and adjusts resource allocation accordingly. During periods of high demand, it scales up resources, while in times of reduced activity, it efficiently scales down. This dynamic optimization guarantees that cloud resources are used judiciously, maximizing cost efficiency and delivering consistent performance.

- **Self-healing capabilities:** Finally, generative AI offers self-healing capabilities.

  In practice, this means that AI-driven systems can autonomously rectify known issues. If a service or component fails, AI can instantly trigger remedial actions. It might restart a failed service, reconfigure components, or shift workloads to redundant resources, all without human intervention. This self-healing attribute ensures that common problems are resolved swiftly, contributing to the overall resilience and reliability of cloud services.

Summary

In this chapter, we reviewed capabilities and mentioned some of the tools that ensure observability, monitoring, and alerting, to enable the continuous delivery of reliable cloud services while minimizing disruptions and enhancing the end-user experience.

Q&A

Q: What is important to keep in mind when defining SLOs?

The following list provides some of the considerations when defining SLOs. Irrespective of the situation, you need to align with your stakeholders and customers in defining SLOs for your organization.

- When creating SLOs, align them with user expectations. For instance, if your users expect your service to respond within 200 milliseconds, set an SLO that reflects this expectation.
- Evaluate the potential risks and impacts of different SLOs. Stricter SLOs might be more challenging to meet, but they provide a higher level of reliability.
- Finally, use historical data and machine learning (ML) to understand the typical performance of your service. This data can inform your SLOs and help set realistic targets.

Q: How do you use GenAI for CRE?

GenAI can significantly enhance your ability to monitor, observe, and alert in CRE by providing a controlled environment for testing and optimizing your systems. It can also assist in proactive issue detection, RCA, and adaptive alerting, ultimately improving the overall reliability and performance of your cloud-based services.

To summarize the content presented in this chapter, the following list represents the most widely used applications of GenAI for CRE.

1. **Anomaly detection:** GenAI models can be trained to detect anomalies in the system's data.

2. **Data generation:** GenAI models can create synthetic data resembling actual system behavior. This can be used for system testing. Moreover, GenAI can be leveraged with chaos engineering to simulate scenarios, such as traffic spikes, resource failures, and unexpected user behavior, and check how a system will respond to these conditions. Some examples include load testing, fault injection, latency injection, region and/or Availability Zone (AZ) failure, and other engineering-introduced chaos.

3. **Alerting optimization:** GenAI may continuously adjust alerting thresholds to provide timely and dynamic alerts in complex environments. It can fine-tune alarms to ensure that there are no false positives. GenAI models are able to continuously adapt alerting rules based on evolving system behavior.

4. **Issue prediction:** GenAI models may predict potential cloud reliability problems based on historical data and simulated scenarios. They can analyze data across multiple dimensions, and identify correlations and dependencies that humans may not be able to detect.

5. **Analysis:** GenAI can support RCA by narrowing down possibilities and assisting in post-incident analysis.

6. **Self-healing:** AI-driven systems can autonomously rectify known issues, such as restarting a failing host or service.

Given these opportunities, companies need to regularly experiment with GenAI to explore different use cases and stay up-to-date with emerging AI techniques. Learning and adapting are crucial in a quickly evolving CRE landscape.

Chapter 6

CRE via Objectives and Key Results (OKRs)

How to Build a Culture of Continuous Reliability Improvements Using the OKR Framework

In this chapter, we will describe the objectives and key results (OKR) framework and provide practical examples of using it to build a culture of continuous reliability improvement in your organization.

Continuous Improvement in Lean

As we discussed in Chapter 1, continuous improvement is a core principle in Lean, focusing on the ongoing effort to enhance processes, eliminate inefficiencies, and create value for both the business and the customer. In Lean, continuous improvement is seen as a systematic approach to identifying areas for improvement, applying data-driven solutions, and rigorously evaluating outcomes. The goal is to achieve higher quality, reduced costs, and better efficiency, creating a culture of empowerment where employees are engaged in improving their work and the overall value stream. By identifying and removing waste—activities or processes that do not add value to the end customer—Lean practices aim to streamline operations, ultimately improving the quality of the product or service. Let's review key Lean concepts.

Kaizen

From a Lean perspective, continuous improvement (referred to as "Kaizen") is a fundamental concept in engineering. In Lean, Kaizen means the continuous pursuit for betterment, starting from the engineering-related process and system efficiency and resulting in engineering empowerment and a focus on the elimination of "waste."

Waste

Waste is defined as any activity, system, or process that does not add customer value. Usually waste increases cost, time, or effort without providing functional or other (e.g., quality) value to the final product, service, or application team. There are seven critical wastes (or "Muda" in Japanese) introduced by Taiichi Ohno, the father of the Toyota Production System (TPS), in the book *Toyota Production System: Beyond Large-Scale Production*.

- **Overproduction:** Producing more than what is needed or producing too early, leading to excess inventory and tying up valuable resources. In cloud reliability engineering (CRE), this refers to creating exaggerated amounts of chaos engineering experiments, service level indicators (SLIs), metrics, alerts, and other performance indicators when your application does not have enough users to know where to apply them. Leveraging an incremental approach to the delivery of results is critical to the success and elimination of waste.
- **Inventory:** Storing excess raw materials, work in progress, or finished goods, which incurs holding costs, takes up space, and

can lead to obsolescence. In CRE, this refers to building *all* the features of a system without considering the priorities of the user. Most users end up leveraging 20% of the capabilities of a given app, so why produce 100% and wait too long to create an early feedback cycle from your customers?

- **Transportation:** Unnecessary movement or transportation of materials, products, or information, adding no value to the end customer. In CRE, this refers to duplicating datasets unnecessarily and creating different systems of record that are duplicative. As we design our systems and create new consumers and producers of data, CRE teams need to consider how to set contracts between systems to leverage a single version of truth and at the same time duplicate only when it is needed.

- **Waiting:** Idle time or delays in the production process, where work is not progressing and resources are wasted. In CRE, this refers to managing dependencies and knowing the impact those can create on your mission-critical applications. For example, you can have the best CRE practices to reduce latency for a critical application (e.g., 50 ms), but if one of the dependencies does not consider latency as something critical for its action, your entire system will be impacted for the wait time that is introduced in your critical app.

- **Motion:** Unnecessary physical movement of people or equipment, leading to inefficiency and fatigue. While in CRE there is no physical movement of people or equipment, there are many factors that lead to engineer fatigue. For example, if your team creates hundreds of dashboards that produce one million alerts per day to track everything that is possible in the world of CRE, this will absolutely create alert fatigue and very quickly demotivate any engineer to have fun and be part of your organization. CRE suggests a continuous incremental approach to setting up things such as metrics, alerts, thresholds, chaos tests, playbooks, and runbook automation, always starting backward from the customer's point of view.

- **Overprocessing:** Adding more value to a product or service than the customer requires or is willing to pay for, resulting in wasted effort and resources. In CRE, this refers to ensuring that you manage your capacity continuously. For example, if your application can run in two regions with two Availability Zones (AZs) with a 125% provisioned capacity, why add an extra region or AZ if this will create an increase in costs, operational maintenance, and data replication?

- **Defects:** Producing products or delivering services with errors or defects, which require rework, cause customer dissatisfaction, and incur additional costs. In CRE, this refers to ensuring that your testing and deployment practices are setting your application team up for success. For example, requiring a minimum test coverage of 90% that is automated and executed on every release, and setting up deployment patterns to incrementally deploy using blue-green deployments and incremental feature rollouts with readily available automated rollbacks, will set your team and company apart from others. These types of investments help you identify errors early in the software development cycle, and proactive measures in production if an error escapes to production.

By identifying and addressing these various forms of waste, Lean organizations can optimize their software factory operations, deliver better value to customers, and create a more efficient and productive work environment for their engineering teams.

Continuous Improvement

Once the sources of waste are identified, the next step is to remove waste through continuous improvement. This requires a structured and methodical approach with clear measurements and regular checks against progress.

These concepts, introduced by TPS and related to manufacturing, were applied to software engineering by Mary Poppendieck and Tom Poppendieck, who discussed the concept in their book *Lean Software Development: An Agile Toolkit*. Their work emphasizes the importance of continuous improvement in the software development process to achieve better outcomes and customer value. Besides eliminating waste, they focus on concepts of optimizing flow from ideation to delivery, empowering cross-functional teams to make decisions and drive improvements, focusing on incremental delivery rather than large infrequent releases to allow for faster feedback cycles, and continuous learning through feedback.

Application of Lean to CRE

All these concepts directly apply to CRE, which has a goal of enhancing the reliability, performance, and efficiency of cloud-based services. To build and maintain resilient and scalable systems in the cloud, CRE needs to follow the same principles.

1. **Eliminate waste:** In the context of CRE, eliminating waste means optimizing cloud resources and reducing inefficiencies. This involves identifying and removing unnecessary instances, minimizing data duplication, and optimizing the usage of storage and computing resources to avoid unnecessary costs and improve performance.
2. **Optimize flow:** For CRE, optimizing flow means ensuring a smooth and efficient flow of data and requests in the cloud infrastructure. It involves streamlining the data pipelines, optimizing data transfer, and minimizing latency to enhance the overall performance and responsiveness of cloud-based services.
3. **Empower teams:** Empowering engineering teams means providing them with the authority and autonomy to manage cloud resources effectively. It involves giving teams the flexibility to make data-driven decisions, experiment with new technologies, and continuously improve the reliability and scalability of cloud systems. A key factor here is to learn from mistakes, allowing teams to test and try without the fear of failure, and using a blameless issue review process in which the entire organization learns.

4. **Deliver in small batches:** In CRE, delivering in small batches translates to making incremental changes to the cloud infrastructure rather than large-scale updates. This approach allows for quicker validation of changes, easier rollback in case of issues, and faster adaptation to changing requirements. The smaller the change, the more certainty your teams have to roll back to the previous configuration and avoid major customer impacts.

5. **Learn through feedback:** In CRE, teams should actively seek feedback from users and monitoring systems to identify and address issues promptly. This feedback-driven approach enables teams to detect anomalies, optimize performance bottlenecks, and proactively respond to potential failures. Product teams play a leadership role in funneling these insights back into the CRE-driven team to address concerns and implement solutions.

6. **Visualize work:** Visualization is a key aspect of CRE as it helps teams gain insights into the performance and health of cloud infrastructure. By leveraging observability tools, such as generative AI (GenAI), monitoring dashboards, and visual management platforms, CRE teams can track important metrics, spot trends, and understand the relationships between different systems. This ability to visualize data enables proactive action to maintain system reliability. For instance, when trying to diagnose an issue, teams may struggle to identify the root cause when the data is scattered across multiple tables from different systems. However, by using time series data, creating dependency maps, and employing OpenTelemetry (OTel) agents to gather and track traffic flows, CRE teams can generate more powerful, actionable insights to pinpoint the problem and its solution. This approach strengthens the reliability and performance of cloud-based services by allowing teams to quickly detect issues and take corrective actions.

7. **Encourage collaboration:** Collaboration among development, leadership, product, and security teams is vital in CRE. A collaborative environment fosters communication and knowledge

sharing, leading to better decision-making and quicker incident resolution.

8. **Focus on quality:** Quality is a top priority in CRE to ensure that cloud-based services meet customer expectations and business needs. This involves implementing robust testing practices, proactive monitoring, and continuous improvement to maintain high reliability and availability.

Application of OKRs to CRE

By embracing the Lean principles, CRE teams are able to build more resilient and scalable cloud infrastructures, improve the performance of their cloud services, and provide customer value. However, these principles need to be quantified and connected to metrics. Given the complexity of the CRE landscape and the directional nature of Lean principles, how do CRE professionals monitor progress against the goals they have set up for continuous improvement? Here's where the concept of objectives and key results (OKRs) comes into play. Let's start by understanding the concept and nature of OKRs.

History of OKRs

The concept of OKRs has its origins at Intel Corporation in the 1970s. It was introduced by Andrew Grove, who later became the CEO of Intel, along with John Doerr, a venture capitalist who worked at Intel at the time. In the early 1970s, Intel was facing intense competition in the semiconductor industry, and Grove recognized the need for a management tool that would help align the efforts of the entire organization toward common objectives. He wanted a system that would enable Intel to set ambitious goals, measure progress, and motivate employees to achieve exceptional results. Around 1974, Grove introduced the concept of OKRs at Intel, drawing inspiration from the Management by Objectives (MBO) approach popularized by

Peter Drucker in the 1950s. Grove modified and expanded the MBO concept to create a more dynamic and adaptable goal-setting framework suited for Intel's fast-paced and competitive environment.

To better understand how OKRs can be applied in CRE, let us review the components and cascading mechanisms of OKRs.

1. OKRs drive continuous results and improvements in a structured and intentional way. According to this framework, there are two components.

   Objectives, which are the qualitative and ambitious goals that an organization aspired to achieve. They are hard to achieve (but not impossible), are tied to the company's vision, and provide clear direction.

   Key Results (KRs), which are the specific, measurable, and time-bound outcomes indicating progress toward achieving these objectives.

   Since Intel, OKRs have been widely adopted and are becoming an increasingly popular tool to achieve progress against stated goals. The simplicity, flexibility, and focus on measurable outcomes have made OKRs a popular choice for companies seeking to drive alignment, engagement, and continuous improvement in their operations.

   Usually, there are three to five objectives for each organization and three to five KRs associated with each of those. They can be set at an annual or quarterly time frame, and the progress against the objective is continuously measured to ensure that the organization (team) is on the right track.

   Figure 6.1 illustrates the structure of OKRs in a typical quarterly cycle. The figure shows a clear "Objective" for the quarter, which sets the overarching goal for the team or organization. The KRs provide the measurable outcomes that help track progress toward achieving the objective. Each KR would have a status update based on predefined metrics, indicating how well the goal is being achieved. It highlights the role of "Initiatives"—projects or tasks that are designed to move the needle forward on the KRs.

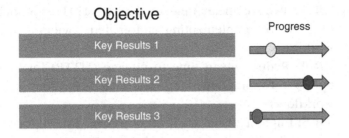

Figure 6.1
Key components of
OKR

2. OKRs cascade throughout the company so that the goals of the company get translated into divisional goals specific to each competency. OKRs should be reviewed and updated regularly to reflect changing priorities and to ensure continuous progress toward the desired outcomes. There are usually monitoring and reporting tools in place (dashboards, monitoring tools, performance tools, and alerts) that provide inputs into the periodic review process (usually biweekly or monthly) where companies can course-correct in case KRs do not show improvement, or if the company is not able to achieve its objectives despite KR improvement. In this case, the organization will pivot and make an assumption related to its ability to achieve the objectives through different KRs.

OKR Examples

The list that follows outlines some of the sample OKR sets for a large-scale company.

- **Objective 1: Improve Service Reliability (Availability, Recovery, and Resiliency)**
  - **KR 1:** Achieve 99.99% uptime for critical customer experience or cloud services in the next quarter.
  - **KR 2:** Reduce mean time to recover (MTTR) for incidents by 25% by implementing automated incident response workflows.

- **KR 3:** Reduce mean time to detect (MTTD) for incidents by 25% by implementing automated incident response workflows.
- **KR 4:** Reduce mean time to engage (MTTE) for incidents by 25% by implementing automated incident response workflows.
- **KR 5:** Implement service level objectives (SLOs) for all critical applications and ensure that applications not meeting the SLO conduct an operational readiness review (ORR).
- **KR 6:** Create a monthly report containing availability data for 56 previously identified enterprise-critical services with an outline of Correction of Error (COE) or problem activities related to each outage.
- **Objective 2: Enhance Scalability and Performance**
  - **KR 1:** Increase the capacity of cloud infrastructure to handle 30% growth in user traffic without performance degradation.
  - **KR 2:** Reduce response time variability for critical cloud services by maintaining a 95% response time within a narrow range (e.g., +/− 10% of the average response time).
  - **KR 3:** Improve database response time by implementing indexing, caching, or other optimization techniques, resulting in a 20% reduction in database query time.
  - **KR 4:** Decrease response time for API requests by 20% through optimizations and caching strategies.
  - **KR 5:** Decrease the error rate of cloud services to less than 0.5%, ensuring that the majority of user interactions are successful without errors.
- **Objective 3: Enhance Incident Response and Disaster Recovery**
  - **KR 1:** Implement a comprehensive disaster recovery plan and conduct successful disaster recovery tests with zero data loss.
  - **KR 2:** Reduce the average time to detect and respond to incidents by 40% through enhanced monitoring and automation.
  - **KR 3:** Reduce the average time taken to resolve critical incidents by 30% compared to the previous quarter.

- **KR 4:** Conduct post-incident reviews for all major incidents within 48 hours of resolution, identifying root causes and implementing preventive actions.
- **KR 5:** Ensure that the recovery point objective (RPO) for critical cloud services is met consistently, with no more than one hour of potential data loss in the event of a disaster.
- **Objective 4: Optimize Cloud Costs and Resource Utilization**
  - **KR 1:** Reduce cloud infrastructure costs by 15% through rightsizing and efficient resource allocation.
  - **KR 2:** Increase the cloud resource utilization rate to 80% by implementing auto-scaling and workload consolidation strategies.
  - **KR 3:** Identify and resize overprovisioned cloud resources to match actual usage patterns, resulting in at least a 20% reduction in unnecessary costs.
  - **KR 4:** Implement a Spot Instance strategy to utilize low-cost, unused cloud resources, aiming for 10% of the overall workload to run on Spot Instances.
  - **KR 5:** Implement automated resource lifecycle management to terminate idle or unused instances, leading to a 15% reduction in resource waste.
- **Objective 5: Strengthen Security and Compliance**
  - **KR 1:** Conduct a comprehensive security compliance audit and achieve a passing score of 90% against relevant industry standards and regulations (including ISO 27001, SOC 2, GDPR).
  - **KR 2:** Reduce the number of security vulnerabilities in cloud systems by 30% through proactive vulnerability assessments and remediation efforts.
  - **KR 3:** Reduce the average time to remediate critical security vulnerabilities in cloud systems to less than 48 hours from the time of discovery.
  - **KR 4:** Enforce multifactor authentication (MFA) for all privileged accounts and achieve a 90% MFA adoption rate within the CRE team.
  - **KR 5:** Ensure that all security incidents are properly documented and reported within 24 hours of detection, adhering to the organization's incident response process.

Please note that these are provided for illustration only and will depend on the company vision, long-term goals, and customer and business issues that need to be addressed at a specific point in time. By implementing OKRs, engineering leaders will be able to align their efforts with strategic business objectives, foster a culture of transparency and accountability, and drive continuous improvement in CRE practices.

Summary

OKRs enable an organization to prioritize initiatives that have the highest impact on customer satisfaction, service availability, security, and cost optimization. Additionally, OKRs empower individual team members to take ownership of their contributions, making them more engaged and motivated to excel in their roles. As a result, the CRE organizations that implement OKRs become more agile, adaptive, and customer centric, ensuring that cloud-based services meet and exceed expectations while delivering value to the business and its customers.

Q&A

Q: Why are operational readiness reviews (ORRs) critical to reliability engineering?

ORRs provide a structured approach to defining, tracking, and achieving reliability goals. They align reliability efforts with business objectives, promote collaboration and accountability, and facilitate continuous improvement in cloud service reliability.

ORRs are a scalable, self-service mechanism to share and enforce the best practices learned from incident analysis without slowing teams down. This is also how your organization retains tribal knowledge and sets up new teams owning older or even newer apps to be sustainable to operate smoothly. ORRs allow teams to perform operations independently, avoid unnecessary delays during critical events, and know how to react when the system is not operating correctly.

ORR questions uncover issues proactively and reactively. These questions also educate engineering teams on the implementation of best practices to avoid the recurrence of incidents by eliminating and educating them on common causes of impact and reduced resilience.

AWS has made available some questions to help you start your own ORR checklists. For more details, visit https://docs.aws.amazon.com/wellarchitected/latest/operational-readiness-reviews/appendix-b-example-orr-questions.html.

Q: Are there any OKRs that do not focus on system parameters?

Yes, there are culture- and customer- (or employee-) related OKRs that we recommend for CRE organizations. These may include the following.

- **Objective 1: Foster a Culture of Reliability and Continuous Improvement**
  - **KR 1:** Increase the average number of implemented process improvements per quarter within the CRE organization by 30%.
  - **KR 2:** Conduct weekly post-incident reviews and apply learnings to prevent recurring incidents.
  - **KR 3:** Organize monthly knowledge-sharing sessions to disseminate best practices and foster cross-team collaboration.
  - **KR 4:** Implement a system for anonymous employee feedback on improvement opportunities, aiming for at least an 80% participation rate and actionable insights from at least 90% of respondents.

- **KR 5:** Establish a recognition program for team members who proactively propose and contribute to successful process improvements, fostering a sense of ownership and recognition for continuous improvement efforts.
- **Objective 2: Improve Customer Experience and Satisfaction**
  - **KR 1:** Achieve a Net Promoter Score (NPS) of 8 or above from internal and external customers regarding cloud services reliability and support.
  - **KR 2:** Decrease the average response time for customer support requests related to cloud services by 30%.
  - **KR 3:** Establish and maintain a customer-centric knowledge base, aiming for a 95% accuracy rate and regular updates based on customer feedback.
  - **KR 4:** Conduct post-incident reviews with affected customers to understand the impact of incidents on their operations and gather insights for future prevention and mitigation.
  - **KR 5:** Set up a Customer Advisory Board to regularly engage with key customers, gather their input on service improvements, and involve them in the decision-making process.

Q: I am interested in implementing OKRs in my organization. What are some of the benefits I can mention to my management to advocate for this framework?

By implementing OKRs, a CRE organization will be able to achieve several significant outcomes that contribute to the overall success and effectiveness of its operations while reducing customer impacts.

- **Continuous improvement:** OKRs are typically set for defined time frames, such as quarterly cycles. This promotes a culture of continuous improvement within the CRE organization. Regularly reviewing and updating OKRs allows the team to adapt to changing circumstances, learn from past experiences, and continuously refine their approaches to cloud reliability and engineering.

- **Clear alignment with business objectives:** OKRs provide a framework for aligning the efforts of the CRE team with the broader business goals of the organization. By setting objectives that directly tie to strategic priorities, CRE leaders ensure that the team's activities are focused on driving value and contributing to the company's success.

- **Measurable results and accountability:** The use of Key Results (KRs) in OKRs enables the CRE team to define clear and measurable outcomes. This fosters a culture of accountability, as team members are responsible for achieving specific results and can track their progress throughout the OKR period.

- **Customer obsession:** By incorporating customer-focused objectives in its OKRs, the CRE organization ensures that customer needs and satisfaction remain at the forefront of its efforts. This emphasis on customer centricity leads to the development of more reliable and user-friendly cloud-based services.

- **Efficient resource allocation:** With OKRs in place, the CRE organization can prioritize initiatives and allocate resources effectively. This helps the company focus on the most impactful projects, ensuring that time and effort are directed toward activities that contribute to its success.

- **Data-driven decision-making:** The measurable nature of KRs enables the CRE team to make data-driven decisions. They can analyze progress and outcomes to identify trends, success factors, and areas for improvement, thus fostering evidence-based decision-making.

- **Enhanced collaboration and communication:** OKRs provide a common language and framework for communication within the CRE organization and with other teams. This clarity enhances collaboration and coordination among teams, ensuring that everyone works toward shared goals.

- **Adaptability and flexibility:** The OKR framework allows a CRE organization to adapt to changing market conditions, emerging technologies, and shifting business priorities. The company can pivot its focus and strategies as needed to remain relevant and responsive to its needs.
- **Motivated and engaged team members:** Clear and challenging OKRs inspire and motivate team members to strive for excellence. The sense of ownership and purpose that comes from contributing to meaningful objectives drives higher levels of engagement and job satisfaction.

Chapter 7

CRE Tooling

*Tools That Support Automatic
Failovers, Automatic Rollbacks,
Automatic Deployments,
Chaos Engineering, Incident Response,
Configuration Management,
Immutable Infrastructure,
and Disaster Recovery*

Proper tooling is essential in cloud reliability engineering (CRE) to maintain the reliability, availability, and performance of cloud-based systems. Automation helps streamline recovery operations, reduce manual intervention for testing scenarios, and ensure that teams can proactively respond to issues. Cloud providers offer a large number of automation tools that embrace these principles and techniques. In this chapter, we will review some of the tools and discuss why they are important in CRE.

Distributing Load and Volume with Auto-Scaling and Load Balancing

Reliability engineering focuses on measuring how resilient, stable, and scalable your systems are. This requires distributing and balancing loads to ensure an "always on" posture for your most critical systems. Amazon Web Services' (AWS) Well-Architected Tool is an example of a tool that allows you to conduct reviews of your applications according to AWS architectural best practices. It provides a structured framework for assessing your architecture, identifying areas in need of improvement, and making informed decisions to optimize your AWS workloads. Let's take a look at how application teams can use this tool to configure and test the resilience, stability, and scalability of their systems.

Auto-Scaling

Cloud auto-scaling is a cloud computing feature that automatically adjusts the number of compute resources (e.g., virtual machines [VMs]) allocated to an application based on changing demand. The primary goal of auto-scaling is to ensure that applications can handle varying levels of traffic and workloads efficiently and without manual intervention. This is where the concept of elasticity becomes a major player in your cloud implementations.

AWS Auto Scaling (see Figure 7.1) automatically adjusts the number of instances in response to changes in demand, ensuring that applications are neither overprovisioned nor underprovisioned. An example of auto-scaling is the dynamic resource allocation that occurs when AWS Auto Scaling monitors the performance and resource utilization of your application. When certain predefined conditions are met, such as increased traffic or CPU utilization, AWS Auto Scaling automatically provisions additional resources based on scaling policies, such as CPU usage metrics, network traffic, or custom application-specific metrics. When demand decreases, it can scale down resources to avoid overprovisioning and reduce costs.

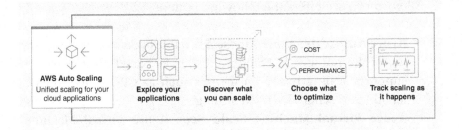

Figure 7.1
AWS Auto Scaling
(source: https://aws.
amazon.com/
autoscaling/; © 2024,
Amazon Web
Services, Inc.)

Auto-scaling also provides elasticity to your applications, allowing your systems to seamlessly handle traffic spikes and other fluctuations in demand without manual intervention. This elasticity contributes to high availability and improved performance.

Finally, by automatically scaling resources up and down, auto-scaling helps optimize cloud costs so that you only pay for the resources you use, which can lead to cost savings during periods of lower demand. AWS provides multiple resources for cost optimization, including AWS Cost Optimizer, AWS Cost Explorer, and AWS Cost Estimator.

GCP provides the following auto-scaling tools.

- **Google Kubernetes Engine (GKE) Autoscaler:** GKE Autoscaler automatically adjusts the number of nodes in a given cluster based on the demands of your workloads. It can scale nodes based on various metrics, including CPU utilization and custom metrics.
- **Google Compute Engine Autoscaler:** This tool adjusts the number of instances in a managed instance group based on the current load. It can scale based on CPU utilization, HTTP load balancing, server capacity, and custom metrics.
- **Google App Engine Autoscaling:** Google App Engine provides automatic scaling based on request rates, response latencies, and other application metrics. It ensures that your application always has enough instances to handle incoming traffic.

Microsoft Azure offers the following options:

- **Azure Autoscale:** Azure Autoscale enables you to automatically adjust the number of compute resources based on demand. It supports scaling based on metrics such as CPU usage, queue length, and schedule-based scaling.
- **Azure Virtual Machine Scale Sets:** Azure Virtual Machine Scale Sets allows you to create and manage a group of identical load-balanced VMs. You can define auto-scale rules based on CPU usage or other metrics to automatically adjust the number of VM instances.
- **Azure App Service Autoscale:** Azure App Service Autoscale offers auto-scaling capabilities for web apps, API apps, and mobile apps. It can scale instances horizontally based on metrics such as CPU usage, memory usage, and HTTP queue length.

Figure 7.2 illustrates how auto-scaling can be configured to create the most efficient and reliable posture for your applications. The figure depicts how the number of VMs will remain at two when the application experiences minimum volumes; as new workloads and users connect, the infrastructure will be elastic to support the additional load and grow from two to a maximum of five VMs. In this scenario, the application has found the need to increase to three VMs based on a condition, whether it be CPU usage, memory usage, or HTTP queues.

Figure 7.2
Azure Autoscale
(source: https://learn.
microsoft.com/en-us/
azure/azure-monitor/
Autoscale/autoscale-
overview/; © 2024,
Microsoft)

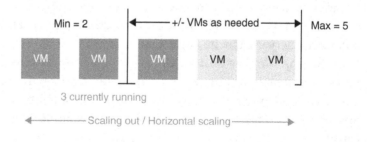

Load Balancing

Load balancing is a technique used to distribute incoming network traffic or requests across multiple servers or computing resources. The primary purpose of load balancing is to ensure that no single server or resource is overwhelmed by traffic, thereby improving the availability, fault tolerance, and performance of applications. AWS Elastic Load Balancing (ELB) distributes incoming application traffic across multiple targets, increasing availability and fault tolerance.

Load balancing includes traffic distribution so that load balancers evenly distribute incoming requests or network traffic across a pool of resources, ensuring efficient resource utilization. Also, load balancers monitor the health and status of services, and reroute traffic (if a server becomes nonresponsive) to ensure high availability by distributing traffic across multiple regions, thereby improving application resilience and performance.

All major cloud providers offer load-balancing tools. Following is a sample of those available.

- **Google Cloud Load Balancing:** Google Cloud Load Balancing distributes incoming traffic across multiple instances or backend services to ensure high availability and reliability of your applications. It offers several types of load balancers:
  - **HTTP(S) load balancing:** For distributing HTTP and HTTPS traffic across multiple backend instances or services
  - **TCP proxy load balancing:** For distributing TCP traffic to backend instances
  - **SSL proxy load balancing:** For distributing SSL/TLS traffic to backend instances
  - **Internal TCP/UDP load balancing:** For distributing internal TCP and UDP traffic within your virtual private cloud (VPC) network
- **Azure Load Balancer:** Azure Load Balancer distributes incoming network traffic across multiple VM instances in a backend pool. It supports both inbound and outbound scenarios and can be configured for various protocols including TCP, UDP, and HTTP/S.

- **Azure Application Gateway:** Azure Application Gateway is a layer 7 load balancer that provides application-level routing and load-balancing services. It offers features such as SSL termination, cookie-based session affinity, URL-based routing, and web application firewall (WAF) capabilities.
- **Azure Traffic Manager:** Azure Traffic Manager is a domain name system (DNS)–based traffic load balancer that distributes incoming traffic across multiple endpoints located in different Azure regions or globally. It provides various load-balancing methods including priority, weighted, performance, and geographic routing.

Table 7.1 outlines Azure's load-balancing methods and features.

Table 7.1
Azure's Load-Balancing Methods and Features

	Azure Traffic Manager	Azure Application Gateway	Azure Front Door	Azure Load Balancer
OSI layer	7	7	7	4
Health probes	HTTP/HTTPS/TCP	HTTP/HTTPS	HTTP/HTTPS	TCP/HTTP
SKUs	—	Basic/standard	—	Basic/standard
Load balancing	Global	Regional	Global	Global
Works at:	VMs	Any IP address	DNS CNAME	—
TCP and UDP	DNS	HTTP/HTTPS/HTTP2/WS	HTTP/HTTPS/HTTP2	TCP and UDP
Sticky sessions	Supported	Supported	Supported	Supported
Traffic control	—	Network Security Group	—	Network Security Group
WAF	—	WAF	WAF	—

All of these load-balancing tools and features help distribute incoming traffic across multiple backend instances or services to ensure high availability, scalability, and performance of your applications.

With sticky sessions, a load balancer assigns an identifying attribute to a user by issuing a cookie or by tracking the user's IP details. Then, according to the tracking ID, the load balancer can start routing all the user's requests to a specific server for the duration of the session. This creates a seamless and stable experience for users, as they will get latency responses similar to those they would get if they were receiving service from hosts and apps within the same load balancer perimeter.

Cloud auto-scaling and load balancing are fundamental techniques for ensuring that your applications can efficiently handle varying workloads, maintain high availability, and optimize resource utilization in the cloud. Auto-scaling adapts to changing demand by adjusting the number of resources, while load balancing evenly distributes traffic to prevent overload and improve fault tolerance. Together, these technologies help create robust and responsive cloud-based applications.

Enabling Automatic Failovers for High Availability

Enabling automatic failovers for high availability is a critical aspect of cloud infrastructure design. It ensures that your applications and services remain accessible and operational, even in the face of hardware failures, network issues, or other unexpected events. The following services play a vital role in enabling automatic failovers for high availability in your cloud-based applications. Depending on your specific use cases and requirements, you can leverage one or more of these tools to design a resilient and fault-tolerant infrastructure that ensures continuous availability and minimal downtime for your applications and services.

AWS

AWS provides several tools and services that enable automatic failovers to achieve high availability.

- **Amazon Route 53 DNS Failover:** Route 53 DNS Failover is AWS's scalable DNS web service. It offers DNS failover capabilities, allowing you to automatically reroute traffic from an unhealthy or unavailable resource to a healthy one based on health checks. In essence, you can use Route 53 DNS Failover to ensure high availability of your web applications, websites, and services by directing traffic to healthy endpoints in the event of failures.

- **Amazon Relational Database Service (RDS):** RDS is a managed database service that offers multi-AZ deployments for database instances. Multi-AZ provides high availability by replicating your primary database to a standby instance in a different Availability Zone (AZ). By using multi-AZ, you can ensure that your database remains available with automatic failover in the event of a database instance failure or planned maintenance.

- **Amazon RDS Aurora:** RDS Aurora is a highly available and scalable relational database service. Aurora Multi-Master allows you to create multiple read/write master database instances for high availability and read scalability. Aurora Multi-Master is suitable for applications that require both high availability and the ability to distribute write workloads across multiple database instances.

- **Amazon DynamoDB:** DynamoDB is a managed NoSQL database service. DynamoDB global tables enable you to create multiregion, multi-active databases to provide high availability and low-latency access to your data. Global tables are ideal for global applications that need to maintain high availability across multiple geographic regions.

- **AWS Global Accelerator:** Global Accelerator is a network service that provides high availability and fault tolerance for applications deployed across multiple AWS regions. Global Accelerator helps route traffic to healthy endpoints in the event of failures or performance degradation, improving the availability and responsiveness of your application.
- **Amazon Simple Storage Service (S3):** S3 offers data replication options, including cross-region replication (CRR) and same-region replication (SRR). These options enable data replication for high availability and data durability. S3 replication is crucial for ensuring that your data remains accessible and intact, even in the face of region-specific failures or disasters.

GCP

GCP provides the following tools that enable automatic failovers to achieve high availability.

- **Google Cloud Load Balancing:** Google Cloud Load Balancing provides built-in failover capabilities to ensure high availability of your applications. It continuously monitors the health of backend instances or services and automatically redirects traffic away from failed instances to healthy ones. This helps minimize downtime and ensures that your applications remain accessible, even in the event of failures.
- **Google Cloud DNS:** Google Cloud DNS offers automatic failover functionality for DNS records. You can configure DNS failover policies to monitor the availability of your backend services and automatically update DNS records to redirect traffic to alternative IP addresses or endpoints in case of failures. This helps ensure seamless failover and continuous availability of your applications.

Microsoft Azure

Microsoft Azure provides the following tools that enable automatic failovers to achieve high availability.

- **Azure Traffic Manager:** Azure Traffic Manager provides automatic failover capabilities for distributing traffic across multiple endpoints located in different Azure regions or globally. It continuously monitors the health of endpoints and automatically redirects traffic away from failed endpoints to healthy ones. This helps ensure high availability and reliability of your applications by minimizing downtime and maintaining continuous access for users.
- **Azure App Service:** Azure App Service offers built-in auto-healing capabilities for web applications hosted on the platform. It automatically detects and resolves common application issues, such as crashes or unresponsiveness, by recycling or restarting the affected instances. This helps minimize downtime and ensures that your web applications remain available and responsive to users.

Facilitating Controlled Deployments with Rollback Strategies

Facilitating controlled deployments with rollback "n–1 stack" strategies is a software deployment approach in which, during a software update or release, a new version of software is deployed to all but one of the available environments. This one environment is typically referred to as the "n–1" environment, meaning it represents the previous version of the software.

The purpose of this strategy is to maintain a fallback option in case any critical issues or unexpected problems arise with the new software release. If issues are detected in the newly deployed version, the organization can quickly switch back to the n–1 version, minimizing downtime and potential disruptions.

To facilitate controlled deployments, cloud providers offer several tools.

- **AWS CodeDeploy** is a fully managed deployment service provided by AWS. It automates the deployment of applications to various compute services, including Amazon Elastic Compute Cloud (EC2) instances, AWS lambda functions, and on-premises servers. CodeDeploy makes it easier to release new features, updates, and bug fixes while ensuring that deployment processes are consistent and reliable. CodeDeploy allows you to define deployment configurations, rollbacks, and monitoring options. It supports various deployment strategies, including n–1 deployments, blue-green deployments, and canary deployments.
- **AWS CodePipeline** is a fully managed continuous integration and continuous delivery (CI/CD) service that automates the building, testing, and deployment of applications. It allows developers to define and automate their release processes, from source code changes to production deployments, using customizable pipelines. CodePipeline supports integrations with various AWS services and third-party tools, making it a versatile solution for streamlining the software delivery lifecycle.
- **AWS Elastic Beanstalk** is a platform as a service (PaaS) offering that simplifies the deployment and management of applications. Developers can easily deploy web applications and services written in various programming languages, such as Java, Python, Node.js, and more, without dealing with the underlying infrastructure details. Elastic Beanstalk provides automated scaling, load balancing, and monitoring, allowing developers to focus on writing code while AWS handles the deployment and scaling aspects of their applications.

The combined value of AWS CodeDeploy, AWS CodePipeline, and AWS Elastic Beanstalk lies in their ability to automate and streamline the entire application development and deployment process. CodePipeline orchestrates the CI/CD pipeline, enabling efficient code changes from development to production. CodeDeploy automates application deployments, ensuring consistency and reliability, while Elastic Beanstalk simplifies application management, allowing engineers to focus on code rather than infrastructure. Together, these services promote a Lean approach to CRE by reducing manual intervention, enhancing deployment efficiency, and optimizing resource utilization, ultimately improving the reliability and resilience of cloud-based applications.

Google and Azure options include the following.

- **Google Cloud Deployment Manager:** Google Cloud Deployment Manager is an infrastructure as code (IaC) service that allows you to define and manage your cloud resources using declarative configuration files. You can define the desired state of your infrastructure in configuration files written in YAML or Jinja2 templates, and Deployment Manager will automatically create, update, or delete resources to match the desired state. This enables you to manage your deployments in a controlled and repeatable manner, with the ability to roll back changes if needed.
- **Google Kubernetes Engine:** GKE is a managed Kubernetes service that allows you to deploy, manage, and scale containerized applications using Kubernetes. Kubernetes provides built-in features for controlled deployments, such as rolling updates and canary deployments. With GKE, you can define deployment strategies, such as blue-green deployments or rolling updates, to control the rollout of new application versions.
- **Azure Resource Manager (ARM):** ARM is the infrastructure deployment and management service in Azure that allows you to provision and manage your cloud resources using templates. ARM templates are JSON files that define the desired state of your infrastructure, including VMs, storage accounts, networking resources, and more. You can use ARM templates to create, update, or delete resources in a controlled and repeatable manner, enabling consistent deployments across environments.

- **Azure DevOps:** Azure DevOps is a suite of cloud-based collaboration tools for software development, including version control, build automation, release management, and more. Azure DevOps provides features for controlling deployments, such as release pipelines, deployment gates, and approvals. You can define release pipelines that automate the deployment process, and include gates or approval steps to control when and how changes are deployed to different environments such as development, testing, staging, and production.

Providing Chaos Engineering Capabilities for Resilience Testing

Chaos engineering is a crucial practice in modern cloud and DevOps environments. Cloud providers developed several tools that offer chaos engineering capabilities for resilience testing, helping organizations proactively identify and address weaknesses in their systems. Some of these tools include the following.

- **AWS Fault Injection Simulator (FIS):** FIS allows you to run controlled chaos experiments on your infrastructure to test its resilience. You can introduce faults and failures into your AWS resources to see how your systems respond. FIS supports a variety of AWS services and failure modes, making it a powerful tool for assessing your application's reliability.
- **AWS Systems Manager:** While Systems Manager is primarily used for managing and automating operational tasks, it also includes features for running maintenance and compliance tasks, which can simulate failures and test the resilience of your systems. It offers a broader set of capabilities beyond chaos engineering, but it can be leveraged for such purposes.
- **AWS Step Functions:** Step Functions can be used to design and execute workflows that simulate failure scenarios and test how your applications react.

- **Chaos Mesh:** Chaos Mesh is an open source chaos engineering platform for Kubernetes environments, developed by the Cloud Native Computing Foundation (CNCF) community. It allows you to inject faults and disturbances into your Kubernetes clusters to simulate real-world failures and test the resilience of your applications and infrastructure. Chaos Mesh supports various chaos engineering experiments, such as Pod failure, network latency, packet loss, and more. You can define chaos experiments using Chaos Mesh's Custom Resource Definition (CRD) API and specify the scope, duration, and severity of the injected faults.
- **Azure Chaos Studio:** Azure Chaos Studio is a chaos engineering service for Azure that allows you to simulate real-world failures and test the resilience of your cloud applications and infrastructure. It provides a user-friendly web-based interface for creating, running, and analyzing chaos experiments. Azure Chaos Studio integrates with Azure Monitor and Azure Resource Manager to discover and target resources in your Azure environment for chaos testing. You can define chaos experiments to inject faults and disturbances, such as network latency, VM failures, service interruptions, and more, and observe the impact on your applications' performance and availability.

Assisting in Incident Response with Automation

Incident response and automation are integral components of CRE, and AWS offers a suite of powerful tools to assist organizations in effectively managing incidents and automating responses.

- **AWS CloudWatch alarms** enable proactive monitoring by allowing you to set alarms on various metrics, triggering automated actions when specific thresholds are breached. This feature empowers teams to respond swiftly to issues and minimize the impact on system reliability.

- **AWS CloudWatch Events** further enhance incident response by providing a real-time stream of system events and changes, which can be used to trigger automated workflows. These events can be integrated with AWS Lambda, a serverless compute service that executes code in response to various events, such as log file uploads or alarms. Lambda functions can be customized to automate incident response actions, enabling organizations to mitigate issues automatically and without manual intervention.
- **AWS Simple Notification Service (SNS)** plays a pivotal role in incident communication and alerting. It allows for the distribution of real-time notifications through various channels such as email, SMS, or HTTP endpoints. During incidents, SNS can be used to leverage application-to-people communications to notify relevant team members and stakeholders, or trigger automated incident resolution processes.
- **AWS Systems Manager** is a comprehensive tool that aids in managing and automating operational tasks across AWS resources. It facilitates the orchestration of incident response activities, such as patch management, configuration compliance, and instance management. By streamlining these tasks, AWS Systems Manager ensures that incidents are handled efficiently and with minimal disruption to system reliability. In essence, this suite of AWS tools empowers organizations to respond to incidents swiftly and automate key aspects of the incident resolution process, enhancing the overall reliability of cloud-based systems.

Google Cloud and Azure offer the following comprehensive monitoring, logging, and diagnostic services that can further enhance the speed and efficiency of incident detection and resolution:

- **Google Cloud Operations Suite:** Google Cloud Operations Suite provides a comprehensive set of monitoring, logging, and diagnostics tools to help you gain insight into the performance, availability, and health of your applications and infrastructure on GCP. It includes features such as Monitoring, Logging, Trace, Debugger, Profiler, and Error Reporting.

With Monitoring, you can set up alerts and notifications to detect and respond to incidents in real time. Logging allows you to centralize and analyze logs from your applications and services. Trace provides distributed tracing for understanding request latency and performance bottlenecks. Debugger allows you to inspect the state of your applications in production. Profiler helps you optimize the performance of your applications. Error Reporting aggregates and analyzes error events to help you diagnose and fix issues quickly.

- **Azure Monitor:** Azure Monitor is a comprehensive monitoring service for Azure that provides insights into the performance, availability, and health of your applications and infrastructure. It includes features such as Metrics, Logs, Alerts, Application Insights, and Azure Automation. With Metrics, you can monitor the performance and health of your Azure resources and set up alerts based on predefined thresholds or custom queries. Logs allows you to collect, analyze, and visualize log data from your applications and services. Alerts enables you to configure alert rules to notify you when specific conditions are met. Application Insights provides application performance monitoring (APM) and application analytics for your Azure and on-premises applications. Azure Automation allows you to automate the response to incidents and events by defining runbooks and workflows that perform remediation actions.

Ensuring Proper Configuration Management

Ensuring proper configuration management and compliance is a critical aspect of CRE, and AWS Config is a robust tool designed to address these needs comprehensively. AWS Config continuously monitors and records configuration changes to AWS resources, providing a detailed history of these modifications. This historical data allows organizations to assess and audit their resource configurations, helping to identify and rectify discrepancies or potential security vulnerabilities promptly.

AWS Config also plays a vital role in maintaining compliance with regulatory requirements and industry standards. It allows organizations to define and enforce desired configurations through rules and policies, ensuring that their AWS resources adhere to best practices. When any configuration drift occurs, AWS Config can trigger automated remediation actions or send alerts, enabling organizations to maintain a consistent and compliant infrastructure while minimizing manual intervention. Overall, AWS Config provides a robust foundation for configuration management and compliance, helping organizations enhance the reliability and security of their cloud-based environments.

AWS AppConfig is a platform that specializes in configuration management solutions for mobile applications. One public case that demonstrates the value of AWS AppConfig and configuration management best practices is its collaboration with a major mobile banking application.

In this case, the mobile banking application was facing challenges in delivering personalized experiences to its users while ensuring security and compliance with regulatory requirements. The app needed to dynamically adjust its features, user interface elements, and backend services based on factors such as user preferences, device capabilities, and regulatory changes. However, managing these configurations across a large user base and diverse device landscape was becoming increasingly complex and error-prone.

By implementing the AWS AppConfig solution, the mobile banking application was able to streamline the management of its configurations and achieve several key benefits.

- **Dynamic personalization:** AWS AppConfig allowed the mobile banking app to dynamically personalize the user experience based on factors such as user preferences, location, and device type. By centralizing configuration management, the app could easily adjust its features and content without requiring app updates or manual intervention.

- **Enhanced security and compliance:** AWS AppConfig provided robust security features, such as encryption, access controls, and audit logs, to ensure that sensitive configuration data was protected from unauthorized access or tampering. Additionally, AWS AppConfig helped the mobile banking app maintain compliance with regulatory requirements by enabling granular control over configuration changes and versioning.
- **Improved agility and time to market:** With AWS AppConfig, the mobile banking app could quickly iterate on new features, experiment with different configurations, and roll out updates to specific user segments in real time. This agility helped the app stay ahead of competitors and respond rapidly to changing market demands.
- **Reduced operational overhead:** By automating the deployment and management of configurations, AWS AppConfig reduced the operational overhead associated with manual configuration tasks and troubleshooting. This freed up resources for the mobile banking app's development and operations teams to focus on strategic initiatives and innovation.

This collaboration between AWS AppConfig and the mobile banking app showcases the value of configuration management best practices in enabling dynamic personalization, enhancing security and compliance, improving agility, and reducing operational overhead in mobile application development and delivery.

Leveraging Immutable Infrastructure as a Service

Infrastructure as a service (IaaS) is a fundamental building block in cloud computing, and AWS CloudFormation is AWS's premier service for managing and provisioning cloud IaC (see Figure 7.3). AWS CloudFormation allows users to define and provision AWS infrastructure resources using a declarative template, typically in JSON or YAML format. These templates describe the desired state of the infrastructure, including compute resources, storage, networking, and more, in a human-readable and version-controlled manner.

One of the primary benefits of AWS CloudFormation is the automation it brings to infrastructure management. By codifying infrastructure definitions, organizations can version-control their infrastructure, enabling better collaboration among teams and simplifying resource provisioning and management. This automation reduces the risk of manual configuration errors and streamlines the process of creating, updating, and deleting resources as needed. AWS CloudFormation also supports rolling updates and allows for the efficient scaling of resources, making it a valuable tool for maintaining a reliable and responsive cloud environment. Whether you're launching a single-instance application or managing a complex, multitiered architecture, AWS CloudFormation provides the flexibility and automation needed to ensure the reliability and consistency of your cloud infrastructure.

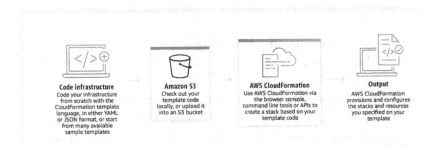

Figure 7.3
AWS CloudFormation (source: https://aws. amazon.com/ cloudformation/; © 2024, Amazon Web Services, Inc.)

Other options include the following.

- **Google Cloud Deployment Manager:** Google Cloud Deployment Manager is an infrastructure deployment service that automates the creation and management of GCP resources using templates. These templates, written in YAML or Jinja2, define the desired state of the infrastructure.
  Key features include the following:
  - Integration with other GCP services such as Compute Engine, Cloud Storage, and BigQuery

- Support for declarative configuration using templates
- Version control and reuse of templates

- **ARM templates (Microsoft Azure):** ARM is the infrastructure management service for Microsoft Azure that enables users to provision and manage Azure resources through declarative templates. These templates are JSON files that define the resources and their configurations.

Key features include the following:

- Integration with various Azure services, such as Virtual Machines, Azure SQL Database, and Azure App Service
- Role-based access control (RBAC) for fine-grained access management
- Template functions and expressions for dynamic resource creation

- **Terraform (by HashiCorp):** While not specific to any cloud provider, Terraform is a popular IaC tool that supports provisioning and managing resources across multiple cloud platforms, including AWS, GCP, and Azure. Terraform configurations are written in HashiCorp Configuration Language (HCL) or JSON.

Key features include the following:

- Multicloud support for provisioning resources on AWS, GCP, Azure, and other providers
- Infrastructure state management and versioning
- Modular and reusable configurations with modules

- **Ansible (by Red Hat, now IBM):** Ansible is an open source automation tool that includes modules for infrastructure provisioning, configuration management, and application deployment. While it's not focused solely on IaC, Ansible can be used to define and manage cloud resources on AWS, GCP, Azure, and other platforms.

Key features include the following:

- Agentless architecture for easy deployment and management
- Support for YAML-based playbooks to define tasks and configurations
- Integration with cloud provider APIs for resource provisioning

These alternatives provide similar functionality to AWS Cloud-Formation for infrastructure provisioning and management, with each offering its own set of features and capabilities suited to different use cases and preferences.

Practicing Disaster Recovery Frequently

Disaster recovery is a critical aspect of CRE, ensuring that businesses can quickly recover their data and operations in the event of unexpected disruptions. AWS offers a range of disaster recovery services and tools to help organizations create robust recovery strategies.

One of the key services in this domain is AWS Backup, which simplifies and centralizes the backup of data across various AWS services. AWS Backup allows users to automate the backup of their EBS volumes, RDS databases, DynamoDB tables, and more. It provides a unified console for managing backups and enables the creation of backup policies, making it easier to adhere to recovery point objectives (RPOs) and recovery time objectives (RTOs).

AWS Disaster Recovery Tools encompass a variety of services and features that help organizations build and test disaster recovery plans. For instance, AWS CloudEndure Disaster Recovery provides continuous replication of on-premises workloads to AWS, facilitating seamless failover in case of a disaster. AWS also offers services such as AWS Site Recovery and AWS Elastic Disaster Recovery (a CloudEndure service), which automate the recovery process to help organizations minimize downtime and data loss.

AWS Import/Export allows businesses to transfer large volumes of data into and out of AWS efficiently. While not solely a disaster recovery tool, it plays a vital role in disaster recovery planning by enabling the rapid transfer of critical data to AWS, ensuring that organizations can quickly access their data in case of a disaster.

AWS DataSync is another valuable tool for disaster recovery, particularly for organizations with extensive data transfer needs. DataSync simplifies and accelerates data movement between on-premises storage and AWS, helping organizations maintain an up-to-date copy of their data in the cloud for rapid recovery.

AWS Snowball takes disaster recovery to another level, especially for organizations dealing with massive datasets. Snowball is a physical device that allows businesses to transfer large volumes of data to and from AWS securely. In a disaster recovery scenario, Snowball can be used to expedite the process of restoring critical data to the cloud.

GCP also offers several services and tools for disaster recovery, including Google Cloud Storage, Google Compute Engine, and Google Cloud SQL. Google Cloud Storage provides highly durable and available object storage, allowing users to store backup data securely with built-in redundancy across multiple locations. Google Compute Engine enables users to create VM instances in different regions and zones, facilitating geographic redundancy for critical workloads. Additionally, Google Cloud SQL offers managed database services with automatic backups, point-in-time recovery, and failover capabilities to ensure data integrity and availability during disaster scenarios. Together, these services form a robust disaster recovery solution that enables businesses to protect their data and applications against various failure events.

Microsoft Azure offers a range of services and tools to support disaster recovery scenarios, including Azure Site Recovery, Azure Backup, and Azure Traffic Manager. Azure Site Recovery provides automated replication and failover capabilities for VMs and physical servers, enabling businesses to replicate workloads to Azure and fail over seamlessly in the event of a disaster. Azure Backup offers scalable, secure, and cost-effective backup solutions for protecting data across on-premises and cloud environments, with features such as incremental backups, encryption, and long-term retention. Azure Traffic Manager allows users to distribute incoming traffic across multiple regions and endpoints, providing high availability and load balancing for critical applications. With these services, Microsoft Azure helps organizations implement robust disaster recovery strategies to minimize downtime and ensure business continuity in the face of disruptions.

Overall, this set of disaster recovery services and tools caters to organizations of all sizes and complexities. These services ensure data resilience, minimize downtime, and facilitate rapid recovery in the face of unforeseen disruptions.

Case Study

To illustrate how to proactively check if your applications and infrastructure are resilient and then optimize them if necessary, let's review a hypothetical case of using AWS FIS, described previously in the chapter, for productively testing applications and infrastructure by injecting faults and disruptions into a cloud environment. Consider Pearl of the Nile, a fictional, successful e-commerce company that relies heavily on its online platform to generate revenue. The company's website, mobile application, and backend services run on AWS, serving millions of customers daily. Ensuring the reliability and resilience of its digital infrastructure is critical to maintaining customer trust and revenue.

Pearl of the Nile faces several challenges related to ensuring the resilience of its systems.

- It needs to identify vulnerabilities and weaknesses in its architecture before they lead to costly outages.
- It wants to implement chaos engineering practices to proactively test its infrastructure's resilience.
- It is looking for a tool to simulate real-world incidents to understand how its systems respond to failures gracefully.

To address these challenges, Pearl of the Nile implements a five-step process.

Step 1. Identifying critical scenarios: Pearl of the Nile collaborates with its DevOps and site reliability engineering (SRE) teams to identify critical scenarios that could lead to service disruptions or performance degradation. These scenarios include unavailability of an AWS AZ; network latency between services; resource exhaustion, such as CPU or memory, on critical instances; and failures in third-party service integrations.

Step 2. Creating fault injection experiments: Using AWS FIS, Pearl of the Nile creates a series of fault injection experiments to simulate these critical scenarios in a controlled manner. For example, it configures an experiment to randomly disrupt network connectivity between two microservices to mimic network issues. Another experiment simulates an AWS AZ failure by shutting down resources in one of the AZs.

Step 3. Executing experiments: Pearl of the Nile schedules these experiments during off-peak hours to minimize customer impact. The company starts with less-critical experiments and gradually increases complexity and severity as it gains confidence in its systems' resilience.

Step 4. Monitoring and learning: During each experiment, Pearl of the Nile closely monitors the behavior of its systems using AWS CloudWatch, AWS X-Ray, and other monitoring tools. For example, the company analyzes how its systems respond to the injected faults, looking for unexpected failures, performance bottlenecks, or areas where the system can be further optimized. The teams also gather data on incident response times and how effectively automated recovery mechanisms kick in.

Step 5. Continuous improvement: Based on the results of each experiment, Pearl of the Nile iteratively improves its infrastructure and application resilience. In addition, the teams refine their incident response procedures, enhance resource allocation strategies, and optimize configurations to ensure graceful degradation under failure conditions.

By using AWS FIS, Pearl of the Nile achieves the following outcomes: increased confidence in the resilience of its systems, proactive identification and mitigation of vulnerabilities and weaknesses, improved incident response and recovery times, enhanced customer trust, and reduced revenue loss due to unplanned outages.

Summary

Integrating tools that help with automatic failovers, automatic roll-backs, automatic deployments, chaos engineering, incident response, configuration management, immutable infrastructure, and disaster recovery into your workflow may require collaboration among product, leadership, and engineering teams. It's crucial to communicate the value of these initiatives to application teams as engineering-driven efforts aimed at enhancing system reliability, rather than mandates imposed by leadership. This approach fosters a culture of shared responsibility for system health and encourages teams to proactively address potential issues. Ultimately, utilizing a combination of tools and fostering a Lean culture of continuous improvement can lead to more robust, efficient, and reliable cloud-based solutions.

Q&A

Q: Describe the difference between rollback or "n−1" deployments, blue-green deployments, and canary deployments.

N−1 deployments, blue-green deployments, and canary deployments are different strategies used in software deployment and release management. N−1 deployments maintain a fallback environment, blue-green deployments offer parallel environments for switching between versions, and canary deployments roll out new releases to a subset of users for testing and monitoring. Which strategy to choose depends on factors such as risk tolerance, downtime constraints, and the need for early issue detection in your software release process.

- An **n−1 deployment** strategy involves deploying a new version of the software to all but one of the available environments.

The one environment that is not updated is typically referred to as the "n–1" environment, representing the previous version of the software. N–1 deployments are often used as a risk mitigation strategy. By leaving one environment running the previous version, organizations have a fallback option in case any critical issues or unexpected problems arise with the new release. This minimizes downtime and potential disruptions. For example, if you have three production environments (A, B, and C), you would update environments B and C with the new version, leaving environment A running the previous version as the n–1 environment.

- **Blue-green deployments** involve maintaining two separate environments. The current production environment is often referred to as the "blue" environment, and the new version, which is deployed and tested in isolation, is often referred to as the "green" environment. Blue-green deployments are used to minimize downtime and risk during software releases. The green environment allows testing and validation of the new release without affecting the blue environment. Once testing is successful, traffic is switched from the blue to the green environment.

- **Canary deployments** involve deploying a new version of the software to a small subset of users or instances first (the "canaries"), before rolling it out to the entire user base or environment. This allows for gradual testing and monitoring of the new release's performance and stability. Canary deployments are used to detect and mitigate issues early in the release process. By exposing a small number of users to the new version, you can monitor metrics and gather feedback to assess its impact. If issues arise, you can limit the impact to a smaller user group. For example, instead of deploying a new version to all users simultaneously, you deploy it to a small percentage of users or instances, monitor performance and user feedback, and gradually increase the exposure if everything looks stable.

Q: Which cloud providers and third-party companies offer CRE tools?

There are multiple tools and services offered by different cloud providers and third-party companies. Often, choosing which tool to use depends on an organization's specific needs, existing infrastructure, and familiarity with a particular cloud platform. Here are some examples.

- **Amazon Web Services:** AWS offers a broad range of services for CRE, including Amazon CloudWatch for monitoring and logging, AWS X-Ray for distributed tracing, and Amazon EC2 Auto Scaling for auto-scaling infrastructure. AWS provides load-balancing services through ELB and disaster recovery with AWS Backup and AWS Elastic Disaster Recovery, helping to ensure fault tolerance and high availability across cloud environments.
- **Google Cloud Platform:** Google offers its suite of tools and services for CRE, including Google Cloud Monitoring, Google Cloud Logging, and Google Cloud Trace for monitoring and diagnostics. GCP also provides load balancing, auto-scaling, and disaster recovery options similar to AWS.
- **Microsoft Azure:** Azure provides services such as Azure Monitor, Azure Application Insights, and Azure Automation for monitoring, diagnostics, and automation. Azure Traffic Manager and Azure Load Balancer offer load-balancing capabilities. Azure Site Recovery and Azure Backup are used for disaster recovery and backup solutions.
- **Third-party solutions:** Many third-party vendors offer tools that support these CRE practices, providing a unified approach to monitoring, automation, and incident response. Examples include Datadog, New Relic, and PagerDuty, which integrate with AWS, GCP, Azure, and other cloud providers.

These services allow teams to monitor, diagnose, and automatically adjust workloads to maintain reliability and performance at scale. Ultimately, the choice of CRE tools depends on an organization's specific requirements, multicloud strategy, and preferences. All cloud providers and third-party tools have their strengths and weaknesses, so organizations should evaluate them based on their unique needs and goals to ensure the reliability and resilience of their cloud-based systems.

Chapter 8

Cutting-Edge Technologies

How to Use the Power of AI, ML, LLMs, and GenAI Models to Revolutionize Your CRE Practices

As cloud infrastructures grow increasingly complex, the traditional methods of ensuring reliability are no longer sufficient. Artificial intelligence (AI), machine learning (ML), large language models (LLMs), and generative AI (GenAI) models are powerful tools that can fundamentally transform how we approach cloud reliability engineering (CRE). This chapter explores the integration of AI, ML, LLMs, and GenAI into CRE practices. We will review how these technologies can be leveraged to predict, prevent, and mitigate failures in cloud environments, ensuring high availability and reliability of services.

Understanding AI, ML, LLMs, and GenAI

Let's start by defining AI, ML, LLMs, and GenAI models, and then discuss how they revolutionize CRE practices.

- **Artificial intelligence:** AI refers to the simulation of human intelligence processes by machines. In CRE, AI can be used to automate routine tasks, detect anomalies, and make data-driven decisions.

- **Machine learning:** A subset of AI, ML involves training algorithms on large datasets to identify patterns and make predictions. For CRE, ML can be invaluable in predictive maintenance, anomaly detection, and capacity planning.
- **Large language models:** LLMs are deep learning models that can understand and generate humanlike text based on the data they were trained on. LLMs can be used in CRE for tasks such as automated incident response, documentation generation, and real-time troubleshooting guidance.
- **Generative AI models:** GenAI models can generate new data similar to the data they were trained on. In the context of CRE, GenAI can be used to design potential failure scenarios, creating synthetic data for testing and validation of systems under various conditions.

Benefits of Integrating These Technologies into CRE Practices

The integration of these technologies into CRE practices offers multiple benefits:

- Proactive issue detection and resolution
- Improved application performance management
- Automated alerting and escalation for incident management
- Security threat detection
- Improved monitoring
- Predictive analytics
- Predictive maintenance
- Enhanced decision-making
- Simulation and testing
- Improved documentation and knowledge sharing

- Cost efficiency
- Improved user experience
- Customer service and support

Proactive Issue Detection and Resolution

AI and ML models can continuously monitor cloud environments, identifying potential issues before they escalate into critical failures. This proactive approach helps maintain higher levels of service availability and reliability.

There are multiple applications of these technologies to proactively detect and resolve issues. The most widely used is continuous monitoring and anomaly detection. AI and ML models continuously monitor cloud environments, analyzing vast amounts of data in real time. These models learn the normal behavior patterns of the system and can detect anomalies that might indicate potential issues. By identifying deviations from the norm, these models can flag potential problems before they develop into critical failures.

For example, a large-scale cloud provider could use AI models to continuously monitor the health and performance of its hosts, storage systems, and network components. In this scenario, an ML model might track metrics such as CPU utilization, memory usage, disk I/O, and network latency across thousands of hosts. When the model detects a pattern indicating a potential hardware failure, such as an unusual spike in I/O wait times coupled with increased error rates, it generates an alert. This allows the CRE team to preemptively migrate workloads to other regions, or scale healthy hosts or refresh hosts in the affected stack, thereby preventing service disruptions.

Improved Application Performance Management

Another use case is related to application performance management. In a cloud-based e-commerce platform, AI models analyze user transaction data and backend service metrics to ensure optimal performance. In this scenario, an ML model might monitor transaction response times, database query performance, and API call success rates. If the model detects a trend of increasing response times and intermittent API failures during peak shopping hours, it can alert the CRE team. The team can then investigate and resolve the issue, such as by scaling up resources or optimizing database queries, before it impacts end users, ensuring a seamless shopping experience.

Automated Alerting and Escalation for Incident Management

Leveraging LLMs and AI can automate incident management processes. From initial detection to resolution, these technologies can streamline workflows, reducing the time it takes to resolve issues and minimizing downtime. When AI and ML models detect potential issues, they can automatically generate alerts and escalate them to the relevant teams. This ensures that issues are addressed promptly, reducing the risk of escalation into more severe problems.

Security Threat Detection

Another application of these technologies is security threat detection. In a global financial services company's cloud implementation, for example, AI-driven security systems continuously analyze network traffic patterns to identify potential threats. In this scenario, an ML model might be trained to detect anomalies such as unusual login attempts, unexpected data transfers, or irregular access patterns to sensitive databases. If the model identifies a sudden spike in login attempts from an unfamiliar geographic location, it can flag this as a potential brute-force attack. The CRE team can then take immediate action to mitigate the threat, such as by blocking suspicious IP addresses and initiating a security audit.

Improved Monitoring

Monitoring can be related to compliance and regulations. For example, in a healthcare cloud platform, compliance with data privacy regulations such as HIPAA is critical. AI models continuously monitor system logs, access controls, and data transfer activities to ensure compliance. In this scenario, an ML model might detect unauthorized access attempts to patient records or unencrypted data transfers. By proactively identifying these compliance violations, the CRE team can take corrective actions, such as adjusting access controls or enforcing encryption policies, to maintain regulatory compliance and avoid legal penalties.

Predictive Analytics

A common application of these technologies is predictive analytics. ML algorithms can be trained on historical data to predict future issues. By recognizing patterns and trends that precede failures, these algorithms can forecast potential disruptions, allowing engineers to take preemptive actions. This predictive capability is crucial for maintaining high service availability and reliability. A cloud service provider operates multiple data centers, each hosting thousands of servers. AI models analyze historical maintenance records, sensor data, and operational logs to predict when hardware components are likely to fail. In this scenario, an ML model might predict that a specific batch of hard drives is approaching end-of-life based on increased read/write errors and elevated temperatures. By predicting these failures, the CRE team can schedule proactive replacements during planned maintenance windows, thereby avoiding unplanned outages and ensuring continuous service availability.

Another example is the cloud implementation of software for a global manufacturing company. This company operates a cloud-based platform for monitoring and managing factory equipment across multiple locations. AI models analyze sensor data from machines, including vibration, temperature, and operational cycles, to predict when a machine is likely to fail. In this scenario, an ML model might detect patterns indicating that a particular type of motor tends to overheat and fail after a certain number of operational hours. By predicting these failures, the CRE team can schedule maintenance during planned downtimes, reducing unexpected outages and ensuring continuous production.

Several examples of cloud implementations in other industries include the following.

- Financial services firms can utilize AI-driven predictive analytics to manage risks associated with trading and transactions. AI models analyze market data, transaction histories, and economic indicators to predict potential market fluctuations and fraudulent activities. In this scenario, an ML model might identify unusual trading patterns that suggest a risk of market manipulation. By predicting these risks, the CRE team can implement security measures and adjust trading algorithms to mitigate potential losses and maintain system integrity.
- Telecommunications companies can leverage AI to predict network usage and optimize resource allocation. In this scenario, ML models can analyze historical data on network traffic, call volumes, and data usage to forecast future demand. The models might predict higher network usage in specific regions during major sporting events or concerts. The CRE team can use these predictions to dynamically allocate bandwidth and computing resources, preventing network congestion and ensuring consistent service quality.
- Energy utility companies can use AI to predict energy consumption patterns and optimize the operation of power grids. In this scenario, ML models can analyze data from smart meters, weather forecasts, and historical usage to forecast demand. The models might predict increased energy usage during a heatwave. The CRE team can use this information to adjust power generation and distribution, preventing outages and ensuring a stable energy supply to customers.

- Large retail chains can employ AI to optimize inventory management across their stores. AI models analyze sales data, seasonal trends, and supply chain logistics to predict stock levels and reorder points. In this scenario, an ML model might forecast a rise in demand for winter clothing as temperatures drop. The CRE team can ensure that cloud resources supporting inventory systems are scaled appropriately, enabling real-time updates and reducing the risk of stockouts or overstock situations.

Predictive Maintenance

ML algorithms can analyze historical data to predict when and where failures are likely to occur, allowing for timely maintenance (using feature flags to test new features, ensuring that old features support modernization efforts) and reducing unexpected outages. In addition, predictive maintenance and demand forecasting can reduce the need for emergency repairs and overprovisioning, leading to significant cost savings.

Predictive analytics leads to predictive maintenance when ML algorithms analyze historical data to predict when and where failures are likely to occur, allowing for timely maintenance and reducing unexpected outages. A use case is a global airline company that utilizes ML algorithms to analyze data from aircraft sensors, flight logs, and maintenance records in its cloud implementation. The ML model identifies patterns indicating potential engine failures, allowing the airline to perform maintenance during scheduled downtimes. This proactive approach reduces the risk of in-flight engine failures, enhances passenger safety, and minimizes costly emergency repairs.

Enhanced Decision-Making

AI-powered analytics provide deeper insights into system performance, helping engineers make informed decisions about infrastructure upgrades, resource allocation, and risk management. As an example, a multinational financial institution can employ AI-powered analytics to monitor the performance of its trading platforms. By analyzing data on transaction volumes, latency, and error rates, the AI system identifies areas where infrastructure upgrades are needed. This enables engineers to allocate resources effectively, prioritize high-impact improvements, and mitigate risks associated with system failures during peak trading hours.

Simulation and Testing

GenAI models can create realistic simulations of failure scenarios, enabling thorough testing of systems under various conditions without affecting live environments. As an example, a leading cloud service provider can use GenAI models to simulate various failure scenarios, such as data center outages or network disruptions. These simulations allow the CRE team to test the resilience of their systems under extreme conditions. By identifying potential weaknesses and validating recovery procedures in a controlled environment, the provider ensures high availability and reliability for its customers.

Improved Documentation and Knowledge Sharing

LLMs can assist in generating accurate and up-to-date documentation, facilitating better knowledge-sharing and onboarding processes for engineering teams. As an example, a large technology company can leverage LLMs to generate and maintain comprehensive documentation for its cloud infrastructure. The LLMs analyze system configurations, code repositories, and support tickets to produce detailed guides, troubleshooting steps, and best practices. This improved documentation helps new engineers quickly understand the system, reduces onboarding time, and ensures consistent knowledge sharing across teams. Some companies claim to have improved developer productivity and platform support by up to 25 times just by leveraging auto-generated documentation and LLM-driven chatbots.

Cost Efficiency

Cost efficiency is another important application of these technologies. Predictive maintenance and demand forecasting reduce the need for emergency repairs and overprovisioning, leading to significant cost savings. For example, an energy utility company can employ predictive maintenance to monitor its power generation equipment. ML algorithms analyze historical performance data and environmental conditions to predict when maintenance is required. By scheduling maintenance proactively, the company avoids costly emergency repairs and extends the lifespan of its equipment. Additionally, demand forecasting helps the company optimize energy production, reducing the need for overprovisioning and lowering operational costs.

Improved User Experience

Anticipating and addressing issues before they impact users ensures a seamless and satisfying user experience, which is critical for customer retention and satisfaction. As an example, a major e-commerce platform can use AI to monitor user interactions and detect potential performance issues, such as slow page load times or payment processing errors. By identifying and resolving these issues before they affect customers, the platform ensures a smooth shopping experience. This proactive approach leads to higher customer satisfaction, increased sales, and improved retention rates.

Customer Service and Support

Multiple companies use these technologies for their customer service and support. As an example, in a software-as-a-service (SaaS) company, AI-driven chatbots and virtual assistants provide first-line support to customers. An AI model might analyze user interaction logs and system performance metrics to identify common issues, such as connectivity problems or software bugs. Then, if the model detects that multiple users are experiencing slow response times when accessing a specific feature, it can proactively suggest trouble-shooting steps or escalate the issue to the CRE team. This reduces the burden on human support agents and ensures timely resolution of customer issues.

Benefits Summary

To summarize, some of the common benefits of using AI, ML, LLMs, and GenAI in CRE include the following.

- **Increased service availability:** By detecting and addressing potential issues early, AI and ML models help maintain high levels of service availability, ensuring uninterrupted access for users.
- **Reduced downtime:** Proactive issue resolution minimizes the occurrence of critical failures, leading to less downtime and enhanced system reliability.
- **Cost savings:** Early detection and resolution of issues prevents costly outages and reduces the need for emergency mainte-nance, resulting in significant cost savings.
- **Improved customer satisfaction:** Maintaining high service reliability and availability enhances customer trust and satis-faction, contributing to better business outcomes. Predictive maintenance and demand forecasting reduce the need for emergency repairs and overprovisioning, leading to significant cost savings.
- **Improved user experience:** Anticipating and addressing issues before they impact users ensures a seamless and satis-fying user experience, which is critical for customer retention and satisfaction.
- **Enhanced operational efficiency:** Automated monitoring and alerting streamline the incident management process, allowing CRE teams to focus on strategic initiatives rather than firefighting.

- **Optimized resource allocation:** By forecasting demand and usage patterns, predictive analytics helps in optimizing the allocation of cloud resources, reducing waste and ensuring efficient utilization.
- **Informed decision-making:** AI-powered predictive analytics provides deep insights into system performance and user behavior, enabling informed decision-making and strategic planning.

Implementation Considerations

As you implement AI, ML, LLMs, and GenAI in CRE, you need to address the following challenges and considerations associated with their implementation.

- **Data quality and quantity:** The effectiveness of AI and ML models depends heavily on the quality and quantity of data available for training.
- **Ethical and security concerns:** Ensuring that AI models are used ethically and securely is paramount to avoid unintended consequences.
- **Integration with existing systems:** Seamless integration with current CRE tools and processes is crucial for maximizing the benefits of these technologies.
- **Continuous learning and adaptation:** AI and ML models require continuous learning and adaptation to stay effective as cloud environments and workloads evolve.

Let's review each of these considerations in detail.

Data Quality and Quantity

Data quality and quantity have challenges that you need to consider in your CRE practice.

- **Data collection:** The effectiveness of AI and ML models is directly proportional to the quality and quantity of the data used for training. In CRE, data comes from various sources, including logs, monitoring tools, and user feedback. Ensuring comprehensive data collection from all relevant sources is crucial.
- **Data preprocessing:** Raw data often contains noise, errors, and inconsistencies. Proper preprocessing, including data cleaning, normalization, and transformation, is essential to make the data suitable for training AI and ML models.
- **Historical data:** Historical performance data is vital for training predictive maintenance models. Ensuring that this data is accurate, complete, and representative of various scenarios helps improve model accuracy.
- **Real-time data:** For proactive issue detection and automated incident management, real-time data is necessary. The system must be capable of handling and processing large volumes of data in real time to make timely and accurate predictions.

As an example, a telecommunications company implements an AI-based proactive issue detection system. The system collects data from network devices, user feedback, and service logs. The quality of the predictions depends on the thoroughness of data preprocessing steps, such as removing duplicate records, filling in missing values, and normalizing data formats. By ensuring high-quality data, the company can predict and address network issues before they impact customers.

Ethical and Security Concerns

Ethical and security concerns have the following challenges and considerations.

- **Bias and fairness:** AI and ML models can inadvertently learn biases present in training data, leading to unfair or discriminatory outcomes. Ensuring that models are trained on diverse and representative datasets helps mitigate bias.

- **Data privacy:** Handling sensitive data, especially in industries such as finance and healthcare, requires strict adherence to privacy regulations. Data anonymization and encryption are critical to protect user privacy.
- **Model transparency:** AI models, particularly deep learning models, can be complex and difficult to interpret. Ensuring transparency and explainability helps build trust and allows for better auditing and debugging.
- **Security:** AI systems can be targets for attacks, such as adversarial attacks that feed manipulated data to models. Implementing robust security measures to protect the integrity and confidentiality of data and models is essential.

As an example, a healthcare organization uses ML models to predict equipment failures in medical devices. Ensuring data privacy is paramount, so the organization anonymizes patient data and uses secure channels for data transmission. To avoid bias, the organization includes diverse datasets from various demographic groups. Additionally, it employs techniques such as SHapley Additive exPlanations (SHAP) to enhance model interpretability and ensure ethical usage.

Integration with Existing Systems

In terms of integration with existing systems, the following challenges and considerations are important.

- **Compatibility:** New AI and ML solutions must be compatible with existing CRE tools and infrastructure. This ensures smooth data flow and avoids disruption to current processes.
- **Scalability:** The integration should be scalable to handle increasing data volumes and complexity as the organization grows.
- **Interoperability:** Seamless interoperability between AI systems and other CRE tools (e.g., monitoring, logging, incident management systems) enhances efficiency and effectiveness.

- **Change management:** Introducing new AI-powered tools requires careful change management to ensure that the workforce adapts to new workflows and processes.

As an example, a global financial services firm integrates an AI-based automated incident management system with its existing IT service management (ITSM) platform. The AI system detects incidents based on patterns and thresholds and creates tickets in the ITSM platform, ensuring compatibility and interoperability. The firm also scales the system to handle increased transaction volumes during peak trading hours. Proper change management, including training sessions and documentation, ensures that staff can effectively use the new system.

Continuous Learning and Adaptation

The considerations and challenges for continuous learning and adaptation include the following.

- **Model drift:** Over time, AI and ML models may become less accurate due to changes in the underlying data distribution (model drift). Regularly retraining models with updated data helps maintain accuracy.
- **Monitoring and feedback:** Continuous monitoring of model performance and incorporating feedback from users and system performance metrics help improve models over time.
- **Adaptation to new workloads:** As cloud environments and workloads evolve, AI models need to adapt to new patterns and requirements. This requires flexible model architectures and ongoing learning.
- **Human oversight:** Continuous learning systems should include human oversight to validate model predictions, address anomalies, and guide the adaptation process.

As an example, an e-commerce company uses ML models for predictive maintenance of its cloud infrastructure. The company monitors model performance and identifies signs of model drift, such as increasing error rates. By regularly retraining models with the latest data, the company ensures accurate predictions. Additionally, the company incorporates feedback from engineers to refine models and adapt to new cloud workloads, such as increased traffic during holiday sales.

Summary

Multiple companies from many industries use AI/ML to revolution-ize their practices, ensuring robust and reliable cloud environments that meet their dynamic needs. This approach not only mitigates risks but also empowers engineering teams to deliver exceptional service quality consistently. Utility companies such as Duke Energy use these technologies to forecast energy consumption to optimize power grid operations and prevent outages. Retail companies such as Walmart use these technologies to predict inventory needs to ensure optimal stock levels and reduce logistics costs. Telecommunications compa-nies such as AT&T use these technologies to predict network usage spikes and dynamically adjust resources to maintain service qual-ity. Manufacturing companies such as Siemens use predictive main-tenance for industrial machinery to prevent unexpected downtimes and optimize production schedules. This list goes on and on.

Q&A

Q: What is generative AI and how does it compare to LLM?

GenAI is a type of artificial intelligence that enables computers to create content such as images, text, code, and synthetic data. It focuses on producing original content by utilizing models trained on extensive datasets. Applications of GenAI, such as ChatGPT, leverage LLMs and foundation models to generate humanlike content. GenAI models employ complex ML algorithms to understand patterns in the training data and formulate coherent outputs.

LLMs are a subset of ML models pretrained with vast amounts of data to understand and generate language. These models are particularly useful in scenarios where users can input queries or ask questions in natural language. The LLM then generates responses based on the given input. A key characteristic of LLMs is their ability to comprehend and generate language, making them critical for applications such as chatbots, virtual assistants, and automated content creation.

One limitation of LLMs, however, is that organizations often have limited visibility into how these responses are generated. This lack of transparency can pose challenges in understanding the decision-making processes of AI, especially in critical applications.

By leveraging the capabilities of GenAI and LLMs together, cloud reliability engineers can significantly enhance the reliability, efficiency, documentation, and user experience of cloud services, driving innovation and maintaining high standards of service availability.

Q: How do I operationalize AI with a CRE mindset?

Before you start, it is highly recommended that you get a clear definition and scope of your organization's use case. Also, evaluate several solutions to ensure that you gather enough facts to decide between building and buying a new technology solution or model. Sometimes these technologies must be exposed to customers. If that is the case, consider the user experience and understand any risks that could damage the company's reputation.

Kick-start the revolution and create a culture of innovation with the strategy and innovation team. Set up a group to lead your company's community of practice, and embrace this initiative on behalf of leadership as a key program to advance technology and drive results in your organization. In other words, create a team that will

- Influence leadership to spearhead the creation of the innovation lab.
- Open the door for the community of practice to innovate, explore, and be proactive about the key use cases for your specific organization.
- Partner with the lines of business to tackle key use cases that represent the best return on investment or solve significant problems first, focusing on short implementation cycles.
- Teach everyone how to fail fast and try again as part of the learning culture.

Leverage technology frameworks or solutions that are repeatable and standard in the industry. If you aim to be up and running quickly, consider using cloud service platforms from Amazon, Google, or Microsoft. Their offerings likely include solutions that fit your tool set and approach to ML models, enabling you to scale as needed without worrying about infrastructure.

With a CRE mindset, once you recognize initial success stories, establish a process to quickly transition those use cases, enabled by connected intelligence, to production. This will make you highly efficient in automated production delivery as soon as you see success.

Define the initial skills your team needs to create AI-driven solutions, enabling the organization to build the knowledge, expertise, and skills to support corporate-wide adoption. For a full production rollout, the biggest area of investment is not the tools but the necessary talent (keep an eye on attracting, retaining, and elevating AI knowledge workers, as there are 2.6 million unfilled jobs in the market). Here are a few examples of roles that will be critical for the success of your AI-driven solutions and teams:

- Subject matter experts with domain expertise to ensure that solutions are worthy of investment
- Product owners to ensure that every investment is treated with an agile delivery mindset

- Data scientists/engineers to mine your data and find the best applicable models
- IT architects to ensure that the data sources are aligned and sustainable
- Reliability engineers to ensure that releases are continually integrated and deployed
- Data science lab operations to maintain and govern the environments

Now that you have decided to embrace AI, ensure that there is explainability and governance as part of every rollout. At this time, acquire the knowledge and create awareness to help teams answer the following questions.

- How can we justify outputs?
- How do we increase trust among interested parties?
- What happens if the wrong ML model is selected?
- How can we scale this? How can we commoditize it?
- What is the return on investment associated with operationalizing ML at scale?

Q: What are some examples of cutting-edge tools using these technologies for CRE purposes?

- **Cloud observability:** There are several prominent tools in the cloud observability space. These tools facilitate the exploration of correlations, providing users with contextual insights. Unlike traditional logs lacking context, observability empowers site reliability engineering (SRE) teams to investigate issues at any level of granularity. By seamlessly integrating logs, metrics, and traces, observability ensures that relevant event data is readily accessible. Through its correlation capabilities and integration of LLMs, observability enhances the efficiency of incident resolution processes.

- **Incident response and content summarization:** Jeli, recently acquired by PagerDuty, stands out as a valuable tool in incident response. Jeli excels in generating real-time postmortems during incidents, offering concise summaries of extensive content. Leveraging both LLMs and GenAI, Jeli swiftly distills key information from incident calls or team exchanges. LLMs aid in understanding contextual nuances and identifying critical points, while GenAI enables the creation of condensed summaries. This combined approach facilitates rapid comprehension and effective incident resolution, thereby minimizing the impact on customers.

- **AWS services evolution:** Amazon's introduction of Bedrock in September 2023 marked a significant development in AWS services. Bedrock offers users a suite of tools for building GenAI applications. Subsequent expansions of Bedrock's capabilities have been accompanied by the launch of innovative GenAI services such as Q, Amazon's AI chatbot. Q leverages connectors to access organizational data and is pretrained on AWS data, enabling it to comprehend the intricacies of AWS services. Whether providing assistance with user queries or aiding in the utilization of AWS services, Q offers valuable insights derived from documentation and the Well-Architected Framework, thereby contributing to operational efficiency. Additionally, Amazon has continued to expand its AWS service offerings, with recent announcements including the launch of services such as S3 Intelligent-Tiering and Amazon Connect Voice ID, further enhancing the capabilities and options available to AWS users.

Chapter 9

CRE Value Stream

How to Build Your CRE Strategy Based on Holistic End-to-End Analysis of Your Systems and Customers

There is a saying that a chain is only as strong as its weakest link. This is correct about cloud reliability engineering (CRE) too. If there is one design vulnerability in the system, it could crash the whole system. To ensure that this does not happen, companies use CRE value stream analysis.

What Is a Value Stream?

A **value stream** is defined in Lean as the end-to-end process that delivers a product, service, or result to a customer or end user. Think of a value stream as a workflow that has a series of steps aimed at accomplishing a goal. Imagine a car manufacturing example, popular in Lean manufacturing. What is the series of steps involved in producing a car efficiently and delivering value to the customer (hence the "value" stream)? It probably includes a set of standard steps: processing customer orders to define the production schedule, acquiring necessary parts and materials, setting up an assembly line, assembling the car's body, painting it, installing the interior, adding the engine and other mechanical systems, conducting quality control, and shipping it to the customer. Each of these steps is important in ensuring that the value (the car, in our example) is successfully delivered to the customer. Figure 9.1 illustrates the end-to-end process to lead organizations toward value creation.

Figure 9.1
Lean principles are the key to optimizing processes and creating value.

CRE as a Value Stream

Similarly, when we define the CRE strategy of a company, we need to think about it holistically, end to end. If we ensure the reliability of our networks but do not protect our software applications from malware, our systems won't be functional and customer value won't be provided. This is similar to producing a nice-looking car with a defective engine. By now, you are probably thinking that your company needs a holistic value stream and are wondering how to establish such a strategy and which factors to consider. The list that follows provides a simple but powerful framework that will allow you to establish a holistic value-stream-driven CRE strategy to ensure the reliability, availability, and resilience of your cloud-based systems and services.

1. Start by defining CRE Objectives and Key Results (OKRs), such as the expected uptime, response time, error time, and other relevant indicators. Consider mean time between failures (MTBF), mean time to recover (MTTR), and other parameters discussed in Chapter 2.
2. Based on your OKRs, define service level objectives (SLOs) and service level indicators (SLIs) that align with your reliability

objectives. SLIs are the key metrics used to measure the performance of a service, while SLOs define the acceptable levels of performance.

3. Identify potential risks and come up with mitigations. These could range from switching to a new network provider, to making major architecture changes to implement load balancing, auto-scaling, security measures, or geographical diversity. You can use chaos engineering, described in Chapter 1, to identify vulnerabilities and root causes.

4. Automate mitigations. CRE principles always include automation. Because the primary goal of Lean is to eliminate waste and improve efficiency, automation is the key tool in achieving these objectives. For example, automation ensures flow efficiency. It includes standardization so that all processes are repeatable. It promotes a culture of continuous improvement via incremental changes.

5. Ensure security and compliance. Integrate security measures throughout your cloud environment to safeguard against potential breaches or vulnerabilities. Comply with relevant industry regulations and best practices.

6. Maintain data integrity. It is important to conduct regular data backups and data replication to prevent loss of data. Conducting disaster recovery exercises helps ensure that your company is able to recover on time and without losing data.

7. Roll out the CRE strategy by creating mechanisms for continuous improvement, effective communication, information sharing, and skills development. This includes recovery playbooks and reliability and observability training sessions, videos, or newsletters that can be initiated by employees on this ground.

Next, start thinking about the reliability pillar, which focuses on workloads performing their intended functions and how to recover quickly from failure to meet demands. This includes key topics such as distributed system design, recovery planning, and adapting to changing requirements.

Reliability Engineering Concepts in a Cloud Value Stream

What makes these concepts specific to the cloud value stream? Well, there are additional CRE concepts that are specifically relevant to the cloud, such as auto-scaling, multiregion and multicloud redundancy, and data backups and data replication. Let's review some of those.

- **Capacity planning and auto-scaling:** AWS Auto Scaling can automatically adjust capacity to maintain steady, predictable performance at the lowest possible cost. Using AWS Auto Scaling, it's easy to quickly set up application scaling for multiple resources across multiple services. Auto-scaling mechanisms will be able to dynamically adjust resources based on demand.
- **Multiregion and multicloud redundancy:** Design your cloud infrastructure across multiple regions to ensure high availability and disaster recovery capabilities.
- **Backups and data integrity:** Implement regular backups and data replication to protect against data loss. Some of the AWS services you can utilize include Amazon Simple Storage Service (S3), Amazon Elastic Block Store (EBS) Snapshots, Amazon Relational Database Service (RDS) automated backups and snapshots, AWS Backup, AWS DataSync, and AWS Glacier, providing archival storage service for long-term data retention. By utilizing these AWS services, you can implement a comprehensive backup and data replication strategy to protect against data loss and ensure the availability of your critical data in the event of a failure or disaster.
- **Leveraging the operational excellence pillar:** This focuses on running and monitoring systems, and continually improving processes and procedures. It includes topics such as tooling, automating changes, responding to incidents, and defining standards to manage daily operations.

Once you implement a combination of these services, you need to configure retention policies, define resilience testing schedules, and continuously run chaos engineering experiments to test recovery procedures and ensure the effectiveness of the mechanisms introduced.

CRE Customer Persona

Now you need to tie your CRE strategy back to your primary customer. You might already have a Persona Library in your organization depicting end-to-end customer journeys. If this is the case, leverage existing data to identify the key strategy to focus on. For example, is it a bank processing thousands of transactions in small batches concurrently? If so, stress testing and performance testing will be the key. If complex processing is required, you need to look at cycle time. Cycle time is the total time it takes to complete one cycle of a specific process or task. It measures the elapsed time from the beginning to the end of a process, including all the steps and activities involved in completing the task. If your customer is a gamer playing a complex video game, you need to focus on application performance, nanosecond latency, and network reliability. When defining your strategy, start with the customer persona and the problems this persona needs to solve. Reducing cycle time often involves streamlining processes, eliminating non-value-added steps, and improving efficiency.

Documentation and Continuous Improvement

Once you collect these inputs, document them in playbooks and recovery procedures, and train personnel accordingly. By using and operationalizing this framework, you will create a robust and comprehensive approach to ensure the reliability and resilience of your cloud-based systems and services. Finally, perform continuous analysis as part of the learning and adaptation process. As always in Lean, a holistic strategy requires continuous improvement to meet evolving business needs and technological advancements.

Case Studies

Let's finish this chapter with three examples of hypothetical companies from different industries that use value stream analysis to guide their CRE strategy: a bank, a leading gaming company, and a content streaming leader. While these examples are fictional, they all are based on real-world practices observed in the financial, gaming, and cloud services industries, drawing insights from case studies and industry reports.

Example 1: FinTechBank

FinTechBank, a major financial institution, conducts a comprehensive analysis of its end-to-end value stream, focusing on capacity and transaction processing from initiation to completion. By leveraging existing data on customer transactions, FinTechBank identifies key areas of the value stream that require optimization. Through rigorous stress and performance testing, FinTechBank analyzes the performance of its banking systems under various load conditions. For instance, by simulating high transaction volumes during peak hours, FinTechBank gains insights into potential bottlenecks in its systems and infrastructure.

This analysis reveals that the most critical points in the value stream are transaction validation and authorization, where delays can significantly impact customer experience. As a result, FinTechBank prioritizes improvements in these areas, implementing measures to streamline validation and authorization processes, such as optimizing database queries and increasing server capacity. By focusing on these critical points in the value stream, FinTechBank enhances the reliability and performance of its transaction processing systems, ensuring seamless banking experiences for its customers.

Example 2: GameX Entertainment

GameX Entertainment, a leading gaming company, conducts an in-depth analysis of its end-to-end value stream, encompassing the entire gaming experience from player login to gameplay and logout. By analyzing player data and gameplay patterns, GameX identifies key stages in the value stream that impact player experience: login authentication, game rendering, and network communication.

Through performance monitoring and testing, GameX discovers that network latency during gameplay is a significant factor affecting player satisfaction. This analysis reveals that players in certain regions experience higher latency due to suboptimal server configurations and network routing. As a result, GameX implements strategic measures to optimize its network infrastructure, such as deploying edge servers in regions with high player density and optimizing network protocols to reduce latency. By addressing these issues in the value stream, GameX improves application performance and network reliability, enhancing the overall gaming experience for its players.

Example 3: Streamflix

At Streamflix, the company's reliability engineering strategy intertwines with its value stream analysis and optimization endeavors. Utilizing data-driven insights, Streamflix delves into viewer behavior and preferences to bolster the reliability and performance of its cloud-based streaming platform. For instance, through exhaustive value stream analysis, Streamflix identifies that users encountering delays during peak hours exhibit a higher likelihood of churning. By meticulously scrutinizing the end-to-end value stream, encompassing content selection to playback, the company isolates bottlenecks and latency issues within its cloud infrastructure.

Subsequently, Streamflix undertakes measures to optimize its cloud infrastructure based on these discoveries. Dynamic scaling mechanisms are implemented to ensure seamless streaming experiences during peak usage periods. Furthermore, continuous monitoring of network reliability metrics and application performance data facilitates ongoing refinement of the infrastructure to uphold high availability and mitigate downtime. This proactive approach to reliability engineering, guided by insights from value stream analysis, empowers Streamflix to furnish a high-quality streaming experience to its users, fostering heightened customer satisfaction and bolstering retention rates.

Summary

Use CRE value stream analysis to ensure that your strategy reflects holistic end-to-end analysis of your systems and your customers.

Q&A

Q: What are some example questions to help guide CRE value stream analysis?

By answering a few foundational questions, you can learn how well your architecture aligns with cloud reliability best practices and dive deeper to start making improvements.

Product-related questions:

1. What business problem is this product trying to solve?
2. What are the business processes that we are implementing with the solution?
3. What are the business drivers for the creation of each major component?
4. Is there a list of key events that are associated with each major component or business process we are putting in place?
5. What are some of the key metrics or OKR/performance indicators that we will be measuring success with and alerting on?
6. How does the product team determine customer impact, and how do we measure customer experience? Are there critical journeys?

Architecture-related questions:

1. What will this application and its infrastructure look like in production? What are the tech stack and major components?
2. How many users are we expecting to support at any given time (minimum, maximum, and concurrent)?
3. What upstream and downstream dependencies have we identified so far?
4. Are we leveraging any existing commercial off-the-shelf (COTS) products?
5. What high-level components have we have identified so far? What is the current definition and development status of each component?
6. What is the expected recovery time objective (RTO), meaning how long will it take for this system to recover after an outage?
7. What is the expected recovery point objective (RPO), meaning how much data may we lose in case of an outage?
8. How many data centers, Availability Zones (AZs), regions, and/or countries will this application be serving?

9. What protocols (e.g., HTTP, TCP) and what ports are specifically needed to operate this solution with internal APIs, third-party components, or future Internet of Things (IoT) devices?

10. How are we planning to load-balance and split traffic among the different locations, AZs, regions, and so on?

11. How often are we trying to test our recovery practices by turning down existing infrastructure and introducing chaos into the system to see how it behaves?

12. Are there any data replication techniques to ensure that our data is not only backed up but also replicated across different locations?

13. How are we planning to route traffic when we see spikes in the different zones or locations? Do we expect any patterns that we need to be aware of?

14. How does our configuration management and recovery process work in terms of building everything from scratch? Are we implementing infrastructure as code (IaC)? If so, what are the details regarding the tech and process behind it?

15. Will the solution operate in an active-active, active-passive, or standby architecture?

16. Will the application be exposed externally or internally to other systems or solutions? What applications will interface externally or internally with our solution?

17. Will there be a production support team responsible for the solution?

18. In the event of having to scale up the system, what specific components will need to be scaled up and how quickly will we need to do this? If so, how?

19. Are there any key business rules or business activities that we need to monitor? Are there any that we need to orchestrate with automation?

20. What key dashboards do we expect to observe and monitor this solution?

21. Do we follow any incident recovery practices? If so, what are the playbooks that exist in the organization?

22. Describe the middleware associated with the solution and its parts. How does data move from point A to point B?

Development-related questions:

1. What is the development tooling used for the end-to-end process, and what tools are used to support this process?
2. In terms of the deployment process, what kind of deployment pattern or technique (n–1, canary, blue-green) are we using?
3. Are we leveraging any CI/CD practices to write, integrate, and deploy code?
4. How do we control the environment management process for Dev QA and prod? How do we scale it?
5. What are the different roles of the people included in the development process, from ideation to production?
6. Is there a product road map that shows different components and events for the solution?
7. Are we leveraging any open source capabilities to accelerate the development process, or are we building everything from scratch?
8. How do we integrate security into our DevOps model and solution?
9. What part of testing has been automated, and what is the testing coverage that is automatic versus manual?
10. What type of monitoring will be enabled in production at all times, and what kinds of conditions will result in an alert? What are the expected time to detect (TTD), time to recover (TTR), and service level objectives (SLOs)?
11. How will we let people know that an alert has been triggered, and how do we plan to page the people responsible for fixing it? Is there a "You build it, you own it" (YBYO) mentality, or does a central team respond to incidents?
12. How does the incident management process work, when will it be escalated, and to whom? What are the incident response TTD and TTR targets?
13. Are there any dev standards that we follow? Are any of the generative AI (GenAI), Copilot-like, or machine learning (ML) models used to build, monitor, and test our apps?
14. How do team members collaborate to contribute to the existing code base?

Q: How can reliability be extended to third-party-provided apps?

When conducting value stream analysis to formulate an enterprise CRE strategy, it's crucial to address various edge cases, including extending reliability to third-party-provided apps. These apps often integrate with your systems but are beyond your direct control, posing a dependency risk. Some companies consider them an extension of their value stream, presenting unique challenges and opportunities for CRE implementation.

To effectively manage these dependencies, consider the following vendor management strategies.

- **Strategic vendor selection:** Prioritize established vendors with proven reliability, minimizing the need for extensive monitoring compared to new vendors with higher risk levels.
- **Well-defined SLOs and SLAs:** Establish clear SLAs to define performance expectations, including metrics such as time to engage during incidents, RTOs, and RPOs.
- **Detailed contracts and engagement approach:** Ensure that contracts contain comprehensive clauses relevant to CRE implementation, covering aspects such as TTD, TTR, regional resilience, multi-AZ deployment, incident response protocols and POCs, change management practices, and game day and resiliency test schedules and requirements.
- **Reporting:** Implement a robust reporting mechanism to track key metrics, incidents, chaos tests, and deployment practices, facilitating ongoing performance monitoring and improvement.
- **Risk management:** Apply standard project management techniques to mitigate risks associated with third-party dependencies, emphasizing proactive risk identification and mitigation strategies.

In addition to vendor management strategies, consider the following engineering approaches to enhance reliability.

- **Chaos testing:** Conduct regular chaos experiments in production-like environments to evaluate system resilience and response to adverse conditions introduced by third-party apps.
- **Abstraction layers:** Implement abstraction layers to minimize the impact of third-party app failures on overall system reliability, ensuring data availability and continuity for end users.
- **Incident response playbooks:** Develop clear incident response playbooks outlining collaboration protocols, escalation procedures, SLIs/SLOs, and financial impact assessments for both internal and third-party teams.

By adopting a proactive approach to vendor management and engineering resilience strategies, organizations can effectively extend reliability to third-party-provided apps, mitigating risks and ensuring seamless operations.

Q: How can we easily define the most critical customer experiences?

When it comes to CRE, defining the most critical customer experiences requires a comprehensive approach that revolves around understanding customer requirements, pinpointing pain points, and ensuring the reliability and availability of cloud services. The key components of defining critical customer experiences in CRE are as follows.

- **Customer persona analysis and customer journey mapping:** This involves creating detailed profiles of different customer segments and mapping out their interactions with the product or service. By understanding their unique journeys and pain points, companies can tailor the approach to effectively address their specific needs.
- **Feedback loops and continuous improvement:** Establishing robust feedback mechanisms enables companies to gather insights into customer experience and satisfaction levels. By consistently soliciting and acting upon feedback, companies

drive iterative improvements that align with evolving customer preferences and expectations.

- **Setting clear SLOs:** Defining clear SLOs for cloud reliability and resilience is essential for establishing benchmarks and expectations regarding service performance. These objectives should be established in advance and refined over time to ensure alignment with customer expectations and business objectives.

- **Incident analysis and pattern recognition:** Conducting thorough incident analysis helps identify recurring patterns and root causes of service disruptions. By leveraging insights learned from these efforts, companies can implement proactive measures to enhance system reliability and minimize the impact of potential incidents on customer experience.

- **Continuous customer support and availability:** Providing consistent and high-quality customer support is the key to ensuring a positive customer experience, especially during critical service disruptions. Tailoring support services based on transaction volumes and the critical availability of services helps prioritize resources effectively and mitigate the impact of disruptions on customer satisfaction.

- **Embracing a culture of continuous improvement:** Fostering a culture of continuous improvement within the organization is crucial for sustaining high levels of customer satisfaction and loyalty. By embracing feedback-driven iteration and innovation, companies can adapt to evolving customer needs and market dynamics, thereby maintaining a competitive edge in the rapidly evolving landscape of cloud services.

This approach combines proactive measures, feedback-driven iteration, and a relentless focus on customer centricity. By integrating these elements into the CRE framework, companies can not only meet but also exceed customer expectations, driving long-term success and differentiation in the marketplace.

Q: As we perform value stream analysis, how do we compare our company's cloud reliability against industry benchmarks?

While this is not precise in nature, it is always healthy to compare based on factors such as industry and company size to create your own baseline. The most powerful benchmark is the one your company creates year by year to determine improvement. Once you baseline your key metrics, you can determine how your systems are performing over time and against standards in your industry for companies of similar size based on your findings through customer surveys, your operations data, incident counts and severities, support tickets, and multiple other sources. Your cloud provider will most likely provide multiple services that help you monitor system performance and gain insights into the health of your resources.

AWS alone provides more than ten services you can use, including the following:

- Amazon CloudWatch, a monitoring service providing real-time insights into AWS resources, allowing you to set alarms and automatically react to changes in system performance
- Amazon Health Dashboard, which provides alerts and insights into the health of your AWS resources and notifies you about service disruptions, planned maintenance, and other relevant information
- Amazon GuardDuty, a threat detection service that provides insights into your AWS account security and alerts you of suspicious activities and potential vulnerabilities
- AWS Config, which provides a detailed inventory of your AWS resources and tracks changes to these resources over time

A combination of these services will provide useful historical information that will help you assess the health of your systems over time, and industry data will allow you to benchmark your system's performance.

Similarly, Microsoft Azure offers services such as Azure Monitor for monitoring and diagnostics, Azure Service Health for personalized guidance and support, Azure Security Center for threat protection and security management, and Azure Policy for enforcing organizational standards and assessing compliance. Google Cloud Platform provides services such as Google Cloud Monitoring for performance visibility, Google Cloud Security Command Center for security insights and risk management, and Google Cloud Asset Inventory for resource tracking and change management.

To connect this approach back to Lean, metrics play a crucial role in Lean principles as they provide objective data to measure the effectiveness of processes, identify areas for improvement, and track progress toward organizational goals. In this sense, metrics help organizations gain insights into their performance, align efforts with strategic objectives, and drive continuous improvement. Once you collect the required metrics, you will have enough inputs—from your customers, both internal and external—to identify the areas you need to focus on. Then, you can create OKRs to set up targets and drive improvements in key areas. It is important to set realistic incremental objectives, continuously measure this data via dashboards, report to key stakeholders, and course-correct as needed.

Chapter 10

Culture

How to Build a
Psychologically Safe Environment
and Culture of Innovation
with the CRE Framework

In the world of cloud reliability engineering (CRE), the culture you foster within your organization will make all the difference in achieving true operational excellence. The CRE culture emphasizes learning, collaboration, adaptability, and customer centricity while making cloud-based services more reliable. It advocates for cross-functional teams working in short iterations to quickly deliver reliable cloud solutions that delight customers and empower employees. While Lean principles that drive organizational culture have been around for several decades, specific application of these principles to CRE is a relatively new domain, evolving with the rise of the cloud and the need for highly reliable services.

Psychological Safety

The most crucial aspect of the CRE culture is building a **psychologically safe environment**—a place where every team member feels safe to take risks, voice their opinions, and share ideas without fear of judgment or retribution. In CRE, we refer to this as a "blameless culture." To achieve this, leaders must lead by example. They must actively encourage open communication, curiosity, and experimentation. Mistakes are not seen as failures but as opportunities to learn and grow. In a psychologically safe environment, team members are empowered to think outside the box and innovate—testing and failing quickly and fearlessly.

Employee Empowerment

The second pillar of the CRE culture is the **empowerment of employees and their ability and willingness to make decisions**. In this dynamic field, decisions need to be made swiftly based on data and evidence. This doesn't mean decisions are made in isolation by a select few. On the contrary, inclusive decision-making is a key principle. Team members across the organization are encouraged to contribute their insights and to question any area, ensuring a diverse range of perspectives.

Leadership and Ownership

In the fast-paced CRE domain, **leadership and ownership** are key. In Lean, there is a concept of "Andon cord." This concept is a fundamental element of Lean manufacturing and production systems. It originates from the Toyota Production System (TPS). The **Andon cord** serves as a visual and audible signal that allows workers on the production floor to stop the production process whenever they encounter a problem or an abnormality in the workflow. Imagine a physical cord hanging above the workstations on the production floor. If a worker identifies any issue, defect, or anomaly in the production process, they can immediately pull the Andon cord to stop the assembly line or the entire production process. This action activates a signal, such as a flashing light or an alarm, indicating that there is a problem that needs attention. Similarly, in a CRE environment, everyone has a right to question resilience, reliability, availability, and other related practices, and to immediately "pull the Andon cord" if they suspect any vulnerabilities in the system. The corresponding mechanism in CRE is the error budget and the combination of insights from service level objectives (SLOs) and service level indicators (SLIs). This is where anyone from the app team, the site reliability engineering (SRE) team, the product team, or leadership has the ability to pull the cord and request with a data-driven approach that an application slows down in delivering new features and invests more in improvements to the service architecture.

Overall, the Andon cord is a powerful tool in Lean manufacturing, promoting problem-solving, employee empowerment, and a culture of quality and efficiency. It exemplifies the Lean principle of *jidoka* (automation with human intelligence), in which humans have the authority to stop the process when they sense a problem, ensuring that only high-quality products move through the production system—in this case, the application offering services to customers.

Leadership includes the art of setting up the vision for the organization, requires wisdom and expertise to offer a North Star for a successful strategy, and ensures great communication for skilled teams to work together to make informed decisions. Figure 10.1 shows the basic leadership attributes that CRE teams need to successfully implement SLOs, be able to invest in the CRE concepts explained in this book, and in few cases have the freedom to pull the Andon cord to signal where major issues require company-wide attention.

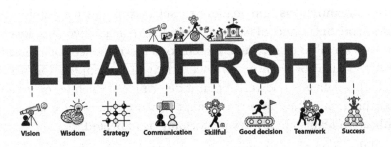

Figure 10.1
Leadership skills to create a CRE culture (image: buffaloboy/ Shutterstock)

Collaboration and Cross-Functional Teams

Collaboration is at the heart of CRE, and cross-functional teams are the implementation of this principle. These teams bring together individuals with diverse skills and expertise to work toward a common goal. As they progress toward this goal, they prioritize customer obsession and focus on maximizing customer value as their North Star. They achieve this goal by thinking end to end versus prioritizing their organizational silos and their own career interests over customer needs. This is referred to as "system thinking." They continuously improve their processes and optimize their practices via learning, sharing, and disrupting the status quo. They engage in direct dialog with their customers using feedback loops as the engine of their continuous improvement, and they are excited to innovate on behalf of their customers.

Customer Obsession

One of the key elements of these interactions is the definition of the most important customer journeys or experiences the company will offer to its customers. In this case, once the experiences are prioritized, the app teams and SRE leads need to inventory the composite set of applications that make up each customer experience. This allows organizations and leaders to set end-to-end traceability and end-to-end SLOs and SLIs. Organizations that achieve this level of maturity are able to measure the customer experience for the enterprise and also for each experience down to the application/service level. This data is so powerful that it determines which teams need to focus on architecture improvements to ensure that service levels and application teams are always performing as expected.

In this type of environment, employees achieve ultimate job satisfaction by delighting their customers, collaborating in a positive and blameless environment, building mutual respect via system thinking, and enjoying their learning and growth in a psychologically safe and respectful workplace. Employee retention growth, system reliability, and availability increase, and customers appreciate the high value and the continuous feedback loop in a trusted and positive relationship. As a result, through people, their engagement, and a positive and collaborative culture, the business grows.

CRE Culture

This might sound like a perfect culture, but it is much easier said than done. A company operating within the CRE framework functions as an open system, continually welcoming new employees to join the conversation and share architecture insights and wins to improve the resilience, monitoring, and observability of their platforms. As these fresh minds and perspectives integrate into the organization, it becomes essential not only to build but also to sustain the dynamic and innovative culture that defines CRE. Achieving and maintaining this culture of ownership, collaboration, and psychological safety is a journey that requires continuous effort and adaptation. While there is no one-size-fits-all solution, there are several strategies that companies should consider to nurture and perpetuate their CRE culture

1. Effective leadership plays a pivotal role in fostering a sustained CRE culture. Leaders should embrace the principles of collaboration and psychological safety themselves. By encouraging open communication, fostering transparent decision-making processes, and empowering their teams, leaders set the tone for a culture where individuals are motivated to take ownership of their work and contribute actively to problem-solving and continuous improvement initiatives.
2. Investing in training and development programs for employees can significantly contribute to the longevity of the CRE culture. By equipping team members with the skills and knowledge

they need to excel in their roles, companies empower individuals to engage in critical thinking and innovation. Offering learning opportunities that align with the values of CRE, such as workshops, hackathons, system design thinking, problem-solving techniques via playbooks, and incident management best practices, can further enhance the culture of collaboration and adaptability.

3. Creating opportunities for recognition and celebration of success reinforces the value of ownership and collaboration. Companies can do this by acknowledging and rewarding individuals and teams for their contributions, whether it is a successful incident response, a creative solution, or an outstanding customer-focused initiative that improved reliability metrics. Celebrating achievements fosters a sense of pride and camaraderie among employees, motivating them to continue their dedication to CRE principles.

4. Maintaining an ongoing feedback loop is essential in the journey of sustaining a CRE culture. Regularly seeking input from employees through operational excellence meetings, dashboard reviews, SRE surveys, incident retrospectives, or informal discussions allows organizations to identify areas for improvement and adapt to evolving needs.

Summary

Sustaining a CRE culture is a dynamic and continuous process that requires commitment and adaptation. Effective leadership, employee development, recognition of achievements, and open communication are vital components that contribute to the long-term success of the CRE framework. By incorporating these ideas into your organizational strategies, companies can build a resilient and customer-centric culture that propels them to new heights in the world of CRE.

Q&A

Q: How do I know if my company has the right culture for CRE implementation?

We believe that the number-one prerequisite for a high-impact, high-empowerment culture in a CRE organization is psychological safety, as it is defined by Google. In Project Aristotle, Google defined psychological safety as "a shared belief held by members of a team that the team is safe for interpersonal risk-taking." By defining psychological safety at the team level, Google emphasized how important organizational culture is to the success of each of its employees.

You may wonder why this research was labeled "Project Aristotle." The answer is easy—it is focused on employee success as part of their team and their organization's culture. In Aristotle's work on metaphysics, he emphasized the importance of understanding the nature of entities as a whole and not merely as a collection of separate parts.

The essence of an entity lies not only in its material components but also in its form and function, which provide its identity and purpose. A famous saying about the whole being greater than the sum of its parts is frequently attributed to Aristotle.

Google's research found that teams with high levels of psychological safety tended to be more successful, innovative, and productive. Psychological safety fosters an environment where team members feel comfortable taking risks and pushing boundaries, leading to improved problem-solving and a willingness to challenge the status quo. Google identified five traits of successful teams.

1. **Psychological safety:** According to Google, psychological safety plays a significant role in promoting open communication, trust, and collaboration within a team. When team members feel psychologically safe, they feel safe to take risks and be vulnerable in front of one another. Google's research found

that teams with high levels of psychological safety tended to be more successful, innovative, and productive. Psychological safety fosters an environment where team members feel comfortable taking risks and pushing boundaries, leading to improved problem-solving and a willingness to challenge the status quo.

2. **Dependability:** On dependable teams, members rely on one another and develop trust via continuous support and keeping their commitments.

3. **Structure and clarity:** An individual's understanding of job expectations, the process for fulfilling these expectations, and the consequences of one's performance are important for team effectiveness. Goals can be set at the individual or group level and must be specific, challenging, and attainable. Google often uses objectives and key results (OKRs) to help set and communicate short- and long-term goals.

4. **Meaning:** Finding a sense of purpose in either the work itself or the output is important for team effectiveness. The meaning of "work" is personal and can vary: financial security, supporting family, helping the team succeed, or self-expression for each individual, for example.

5. **Impact:** The results of one's work, the subjective judgment that your work is making a difference, are important for teams. Seeing that one's work is contributing to the organization's goals can help reveal impact.

We believe that promoting these five traits will create a solid foundation for the organizational culture, which will promote CREs via open conversations, transparency, clear expectations, and collaboration, and allow employees to see the impact of the work that they do every day on the resilience, availability, and security of their systems and applications, and through those, on their customer experience overall. If this does not happen, employees are not encouraged to share any failures resulting in delays in dealing with system inefficiencies or service disruptions. This results in skilled and dedicated high-performing employees leaving and teams not gelling. The outcomes are disastrous to the organization, its business, and its customers.

Q: What are some techniques to spread CRE culture across an organization?

We would like to focus on the fundamental drivers of cultural change within organizations. Start the change by sharing the values and benefits, inspiring people within the company, getting buy-in from leadership, and creating a group of champions or ambassadors of your company's CRE movement. Develop training, set up OKRs, and show the value. And do not forget to add gamification and fun via hackathons and cool experimentation projects that spark new thinking and empower innovation within your psychologically safe culture. In this way, your CRE culture will sustain itself and continuously improve.

Chapter 11

The Business Case for CRE

*How to Measure ROI,
Ensure Customer Satisfaction,
and Promote Business Success*

Cloud reliability engineering (CRE) is not a choice for companies nowadays, it's an imperative. In this chapter, we will explore both the value it brings to businesses and the unparalleled benefits it delivers to customers.

Benefits of CRE

First, CRE provides value by streamlining manual operations, optimizing resources with automated tools, and minimizing costly downtime. With CRE practices in place, organizations experience improved operational efficiency, reduced waste, and increased productivity. By empowering cross-functional collaborative teams, CRE encourages faster decision-making, rapid incident response, and continuous improvement. Companies retain their high-performing employees by promoting a collaborative, psychologically safe environment. As a result, businesses can enhance their agility and responsiveness to meet ever-changing market demands.

CRE Value

CRE is extremely important from a customer perspective. Customers, now more than ever, demand seamless and reliable digital experiences. CRE addresses these customer needs by ensuring high availability, minimal disruptions, and prompt incident resolution. With a resilient IT infrastructure, customers can access products and services without interruptions, fostering trust and loyalty. Additionally, CRE empowers businesses to deliver rapid updates and feature enhancements, catering to customer preferences, staying ahead of competitors, and establishing short feedback loops and rapid response.

To ensure success, it is important to measure return on investment and use the objectives and key results (OKR) framework to ensure that your CRE implementation helps achieve business objectives (see Figure 11.1). Measuring CRE's return on investment involves assessing various factors, such as reduced operational costs, increased revenue due to improved customer satisfaction, and enhanced resource utilization. Key performance indicators (KPIs), including mean time to detect (MTTD) and mean time to recover (MTTR), provide insights into system reliability and incident response efficiency. Furthermore, customer feedback surveys and Net Promoter Scores (NPS) gauge customer satisfaction, demonstrating the impact of CRE on customer value.

While OKRs provide a framework for aligning team efforts with broader business objectives, they don't encompass every metric that matters for product health and reliability. Teams must define their own specific product metrics—some aligned with OKRs and others tailored to the unique characteristics of their systems. This is where the "You build it, you own it" (YBYO) model becomes essential. YBYO fosters a culture of accountability, where teams take end-to-end responsibility for the products or services they create, ensuring ongoing reliability and performance. For a deeper dive into implementing YBYO and aligning it with OKRs, refer to Question 1 at the end of this chapter.

In addition, large language models (LLMs) are revolutionizing how playbooks are authored and used and how documentation and

Figure 11.1
The value of CRE
must be evaluated
using OKRs and KPIs
(image: iQoncept/
Shutterstock)

training materials are produced. LLMs will be playing a continuously increasing role in CRE governance, implementation, and socialization, and they will serve as the foundation in building and enhancing CRE models within organizations.

In summary, CRE fosters reliability, availability, and resilience in IT infrastructure, driving customer satisfaction and ensuring long-term business success.

Cost of Neglecting CRE Practices

Organizations that neglect CRE practices risk facing severe consequences, such as frequent system outages, prolonged downtime, and dissatisfied customers. Without a resilient IT infrastructure, businesses could lose market share to competitors that can offer a more reliable digital experience. Additionally, mounting operational costs due to reactive maintenance and inefficient resource utilization can significantly impact the bottom line. To avoid the pitfalls of neglecting CRE, organizations must prioritize its implementation as a core business strategy. By adopting CRE principles, fostering a culture of continuous improvement, and empowering cross-functional teams, businesses can build a resilient and customer-centric IT infrastructure. Embracing automation, proactive monitoring, and incident response practices will ensure business continuity and customer satisfaction.

Aligning CRE with Strategic Objectives

Once your organization decides to invest in CRE, you need to align the development process with customer requirements (frequently expressed as "user stories") and strategic objectives to ensure that the final products not only meet customer expectations but also contribute to the overall success of the organization. Some key strategies to achieve this goal are as follows.

1. **Customer-centric approach:** Begin by gaining a deep understanding of your customers' needs, pain points, and preferences. Engage with customers through surveys, feedback sessions, and user testing to gather valuable insights. Analyze customer data and behaviors to identify patterns and trends. Use this knowledge to guide product development decisions and prioritize features that address customer demands.

2. **Lean product development:** Adopt Lean principles in the product development process. Embrace a build-measure-learn approach, in which you iteratively create minimum lovable products (MLPs), measure their impact, gather feedback, and then make data-driven decisions to iterate and improve the product. This iterative approach allows you to quickly respond to customer feedback and rapidly evolve the product to better meet customers' needs.

3. **Value stream mapping:** Utilize value stream mapping to identify and streamline the end-to-end product development process. Identify bottlenecks, unnecessary steps, or resource wastage that can hinder product development efficiency. By optimizing the value stream, you can more effectively allocate resources and more quickly deliver products to the market.

4. **Cross-functional collaboration:** Encourage collaboration among different teams within the organization, including product development, engineering, operations, and customer support. Cross-functional teams can work together to align product development efforts with business objectives. This approach ensures that resources are allocated in a way that prioritizes customer value and aligns with the overall business strategy.

5. **Prioritization frameworks:** Implement clear and transparent prioritization frameworks that consider both customer impact and business value. Use data and customer feedback to rank features and initiatives based on their potential to delight customers and drive business growth. This approach ensures that limited resources are directed toward the most impactful projects.

6. **Test and validate hypotheses:** Frame product development as a series of hypotheses that need validation. Use Lean startup methodologies to create experiments and tests that measure customer response and validate assumptions. This approach reduces the risk of resource waste on features that might not resonate with customers.

7. **Monitor and adapt:** Continuously monitor product performance and customer feedback after launch. Use real-time data to understand how customers are engaging with the product and whether it's meeting their needs. Be prepared to adapt and make improvements based on this feedback.

By incorporating these strategies into CRE practices, organizations can create products that not only delight customers but also align with business goals and efficiently allocate enterprise resources. However, once you achieve the balance shown by your initial set of investments, it does not mean that your CRE journey is complete. CRE requires continual engineering improvements, and you will notice that as your team makes improvements in some engineering practices, organically it will recognize new "opportunities" that were hidden or unattended.

Evolution of CRE Practices

The world of CRE is rapidly evolving. CRE companies are continuously utilizing new and emerging trends in technology. Serverless computing, edge computing, and artificial intelligence (AI)–driven reliability are some examples of evolving technologies that companies small and large need to embrace to unlock significant business and customer value in implementing CRE and focusing on the tangible benefits these technologies offer to businesses and their customers.

Serverless Computing

Serverless computing is a technology that helps companies build secure and reliable applications. It frees up time for internal teams by eliminating the need to provision, scale, and patch infrastructure. For example, Amazon Web Services (AWS) Serverless Application Repository enables teams, organizations, and individual developers to store and share reusable serverless applications and easily assemble and deploy serverless architectures in powerful new ways, subsequently increasing the reliability of their systems. The service implements common request/response patterns, makes use of event-driven systems for asynchronous processing, and uses a component architecture to reduce coupling and improve scaling dimensions.

Edge Computing and Distributed Reliability

As applications become more distributed and global, edge computing is emerging as a key technology for enhancing reliability and performance. By processing data closer to its source, edge computing reduces latency and improves fault tolerance by distributing work-loads across various locations. For companies adopting edge computing, the risk of central failures is minimized, ensuring that critical services remain operational even during outages in core systems. CRE practices at the edge focus on reliability at scale, ensuring continuous availability, load balancing, and seamless user experiences even under variable network conditions. Platforms such as AWS Greengrass, Azure IoT Edge, and Google Cloud IoT Edge enable businesses to integrate edge computing into their infrastructures, further enhancing resilience and scalability.

AI-Driven Reliability

AI is transforming the way companies manage reliability, enabling proactive monitoring and prediction of potential system failures before they occur. AI-driven tools can analyze historical data and system behaviors to forecast outages, optimize resource allocation, and automate responses to incidents. For example, AI-powered systems can detect performance anomalies in real time and automatically trigger failover mechanisms, reducing downtime and improving recovery times. Solutions such as AWS DevOps Guru, Google Cloud AI, and Azure AI provide advanced capabilities for improving service reliability through predictive analysis and automation. Integrating AI into CRE practices enables organizations to minimize human error, optimize system uptime, and continuously learn from operational data to enhance future performance.

Scalability through Microservices and Containerization

Reliability at scale is one of the core challenges CRE addresses, and microservices architecture and containerization are key technologies driving this evolution. By breaking applications into smaller, independent services, companies can deploy and manage each service individually, making systems more fault-tolerant and scalable.

Tools such as Kubernetes, Docker, and AWS Elastic Container Service (ECS) provide seamless orchestration and management of containers, ensuring reliability even when individual components fail. This modular approach helps maintain high availability and resilience, as services can automatically reroute traffic, scale, or restart without affecting the entire application. The dynamic nature of containerized environments combined with CRE principles ensures better resource utilization, faster recovery times, and more robust systems.

Infrastructure as Code and Observability

The future of CRE lies in the continuous integration of emerging technologies and operational practices. To remain competitive, organizations must adopt Infrastructure as Code (IaC), automation, and observability as core components of their reliability strategy. Tools such as AWS CloudFormation, Terraform, and Pulumi enable automated infrastructure management, reducing manual intervention and lowering the risk of configuration drift. Observability tools, such as Prometheus and Grafana, provide real-time insights into the health and performance of systems, enabling teams to monitor, detect, and resolve issues more quickly. Embracing these best practices ensures that systems are not only reliable today but also prepared for the future demands of cloud-based applications.

Case Studies

Nordstrom, a well-known American fashion retailer, has embraced serverless computing and has been at the forefront of CRE practices. As part of its IT strategy, Nordstrom embarked on a journey to modernize its infrastructure and streamline its development and deployment processes. It adopted a serverless architecture for many of its applications, taking advantage of AWS Lambda, API Gateway, and other serverless services. This move allowed Nordstrom to focus on building and delivering value to customers rather than managing infrastructure. The benefits of serverless computing allowed Nordstrom to reduce operational overhead and automate scaling, enabling Nordstrom's applications to handle any level of traffic without manual intervention. This resulted in fewer incidents related to capacity issues, as the infrastructure adapted to changing usage patterns. It also increased fault tolerance, enabling the CRE team to design and implement applications with greater resilience, thereby reducing the likelihood of systemwide outages.

With serverless computing, Nordstrom pays only for the actual compute resources used during function execution. This pay-as-you-go model can result in cost savings compared to traditional server-based approaches. The CRE team can then allocate more resources to proactive reliability measures, such as implementing monitoring and alerting systems. In sum, Nordstrom's adoption of serverless computing has significantly empowered its CRE practices. By leveraging serverless services, it reduced operational overhead, improved fault tolerance, accelerated development cycles, and optimized costs.

In the healthcare industry, Moderna uses a broad range of AWS services to support every aspect of its digital, data-driven operations, with the goal of reducing the time and cost of bringing new life-saving therapies to market. Moderna has demonstrated the power of its cloud-based strategy in the speed with which it delivered its highly effective COVID-19 vaccine and its capacity to scale production globally. From leveraging on-demand compute power and machine learning (ML) to accelerate discovery and development to building flexible capacity and real-time analytics providing CRE for its award-winning, cloud-native manufacturing facility, Moderna leverages the scale, reliability, and performance of AWS to expand the possibilities of its mRNA platform and create a new generation of medicines.

Summary

In this chapter, we reviewed the imperative nature of continuous CRE in today's business landscape. CRE brings value to organizations, ranging from streamlined operations and enhanced productivity to customer satisfaction and loyalty. Through the lens of both the business and customer perspectives, CRE emerges as a fundamental strategy for fostering reliability, availability, and resilience in IT infrastructure, thereby ensuring long-term business success. We highlighted essential strategies for aligning CRE practices with customer requirements and strategic objectives. By adopting a customer-centric approach, embracing Lean product development principles, and fostering cross-functional collaboration, organizations can deliver products and services that not only meet customer expectations but also contribute to overall business success.

Looking ahead, the world of CRE continues to evolve, with emerging technologies such as serverless computing, edge computing, and AI-driven reliability offering new avenues for innovation and value creation. The Nordstrom and Moderna case studies in this chapter exemplify the transformative potential of these technologies in enhancing operational efficiency, accelerating innovation, and driving business growth. In essence, CRE represents a dynamic and essential discipline for modern businesses seeking to thrive in an increasingly competitive and digital-centric environment. As organizations continue to prioritize reliability, resilience, and customer satisfaction, CRE will remain a key to their strategic initiatives, guiding them toward sustainable growth and success in the digital age.

Q&A

Q: What does the acronym YBYO mean from a cloud product and services ownership perspective, and why is it relevant?

Company culture is unique to your organization: your philosophy, your vision, the people who work in your company, your leadership, and your people principles. However, there are some approaches to organizational structure and specific principles that drive the culture of responsibility and accountability across companies. The "You build it, you own it" (YBYO) approach is one of them.

YBYO is a culture or governance model in which individuals or teams are responsible for the end-to-end ownership of the products, services, or projects they create or develop. This is opposed to the model in which one group builds new infrastructures, services, and applications and another group (a maintenance or support organization) is responsible for supporting them. In the latter case, the first group is not incentivized to ensure high CRE standards, because once a cloud application is built and deployed to production, it moves to support teams after a short maintenance period during which they do not need to deal with low CRE parameters resulting from poor architecture, insufficient funding, or inadequate monitoring and alerting. With the YBYO approach, the same group is responsible for lifecycle maintenance and support, so from the very beginning, they need to think long term, and they have a vested interest in establishing high CRE standards from the moment they start working on the application.

What does it mean in the context of CRE? With the YBYO approach, the team that builds applications for the cloud, makes infrastructure decisions, or decides on cloud services provision is responsible for overall success, resilience, and performance. This team becomes accountable for the outcome and results of their work, including meeting the company's standards and service level indicators (SLIs), and progressing toward key results as defined in their OKRs. From a Lean perspective, YBYO encourages continuous improvement and learning within the teams, as they are the ones directly experiencing any consequences of their decisions. Within this ownership comes both the potential rewards of success and accountability for any failures. This motivates team members to strive for excellence and take well-calculated risks as required. Many companies adopt YBYO as part of this culture as opposed to one team building new software, designing new infrastructure, making major CRE-impacting decisions, and throwing it over the wall to a different team to maintain, support, and deal with any issues that might arise.

Q: What low-effort, high-impact actions can I take now to increase CRE maturity at my company?

Increasing CRE maturity within your company doesn't always require complex and time-consuming initiatives. There are several actions that you can take now to make a significant impact on your CRE journey. These actions focus on maximizing efficiency, optimizing processes, and enhancing collaboration. Let's explore some of these actionable steps.

- **Conduct game days regularly:** Game days, inspired by chaos engineering principles, involve simulating real-world failure scenarios in a controlled environment. By organizing these simulations, you can identify potential weak points in your infrastructure and applications while fostering a culture of resilience and preparedness among your team. Game days provide a low-effort, high-impact approach to uncovering vulnerabilities and refining incident response procedures, ensuring that your team is well prepared to handle unexpected challenges in a proactive and confident manner.
- **Implement incident postmortems:** Are you learning from past incidents? Conducting incident postmortems is a low-effort, high-impact action. Analyze the root causes of incidents, identify areas for improvement, and share lessons learned across teams. This helps prevent recurring issues, promoting a culture of continuous learning and improvement. At Amazon, there is a Correction of Error (COE) mechanism that follows each incident when the team is analyzing the impact, identifying the root cause, and committing to a set of action items to ensure that this (or a similar) incident will never happen again.
- **Automate routine tasks:** Look for repetitive tasks that consume valuable time and resources. Consider automating routine operations, such as deployment processes, monitoring, and configuration management. Automation frees up your team to focus on more strategic and innovative tasks, boosting efficiency and productivity.

- **Implement OKRs for your reliability initiatives:** Define clear and measurable objectives that align with your company's overall business goals, such as reducing downtime, improving incident response times, or enhancing customer satisfaction. Set key results that provide specific metrics to track progress and success. OKRs create a focused and data-driven approach to prioritize and allocate resources effectively. By setting achievable yet ambitious goals, your team will be motivated to work collaboratively and innovate to achieve them, driving a significant impact on your CRE maturity with relatively low effort.
- **Establish service level objectives (SLOs):** Set clear and achievable SLOs to measure service performance. Having quantifiable targets enables your teams to focus on delivering reliable services aligned with customer expectations. SLOs also aid in prioritizing efforts and resources to meet critical service-level requirements.
- **Encourage and adopt code reviews and pair programming:** Collaborative practices such as code reviews and pair programming improve code quality, foster knowledge sharing, and enhance team dynamics. The cumulative effect of collective expertise strengthens your CRE capabilities.
- **Enhance monitoring and alerting:** Fine-tune your monitoring and alerting systems to focus on actionable insights. Ensure that alerts are relevant, are well-documented, and trigger timely responses. This leads to faster incident detection and resolution, reducing downtime and customer impact.
- **Foster and embrace a blameless culture:** A blameless culture encourages open communication and transparency. When team members feel safe to share ideas and feedback, they are more likely to take ownership of challenges and contribute to innovative solutions.
- **Invest in training and skills development:** Strengthen your team's expertise through targeted training programs and skills development. A well-trained team is better equipped to handle complex challenges and is more likely to drive CRE maturity forward.

- **Leverage cloud services:** Take advantage of cloud provider services, such as AWS Elastic Compute Cloud (EC2), Amazon Relational Database Service (RDS), Amazon Simple Storage Service (S3), AWS Lambda, Amazon CloudFront, Amazon Aurora, Amazon Elastic Container Service (AWS ECS), and many others, that offer built-in reliability features. Utilize managed database services, auto-scaling, and load balancing to reduce operational overhead and enhance system resilience.

By taking these actions, you can swiftly elevate your company's CRE maturity and position your organization for long-term success. Remember that the journey to CRE excellence is incremental, and every small step counts toward building a reliable, customer-centric cloud infrastructure.

Q: What is the future of CRE?

As the digital landscape continues to evolve at a rapid pace, so does the future of Lean CRE. Emerging trends, driven by advancements in technology and customer expectations, are reshaping the CRE landscape, presenting new opportunities and challenges for organizations aiming to deliver unparalleled reliability and customer-centric services.

We believe that the key technology trends, such as serverless computing, edge computing, and LLM applications, will shape the future of CRE. From an organizational culture perspective, businesses will adapt to embrace a more resilient, agile, and innovative cloud reliability paradigm.

The future of CRE includes the following.

- **Serverless computing:** Serverless computing, characterized by the dynamic allocation of cloud resources without the need for server management, will significantly impact CRE practices. With serverless architectures, organizations can achieve enhanced scalability, cost efficiency, and reduced operational complexity. In the future, CRE teams will leverage serverless computing to build robust and auto-scaling applications, enabling them to respond swiftly to fluctuating workloads and customer demands. This trend will emphasize the need for automated monitoring and incident management, where AI-driven reliability solutions play a critical role in proactively detecting and mitigating issues, ensuring seamless customer experiences.

- **Edge computing:** Edge computing, designed to bring compute capabilities closer to end users and devices, presents new challenges and opportunities for CRE. As organizations embrace edge computing to reduce latency and enhance data processing efficiency, CRE teams will need to adopt a distributed approach to manage and monitor the extended infrastructure. Real-time analytics and predictive maintenance become vital in edge environments, where any downtime can have significant consequences. The cultural shift to decentralized, cross-functional collaboration will be essential to ensure seamless integration between cloud and edge services, maintaining reliability and customer centricity.

- **LLM applications and AI-driven reliability:** The rise of LLM applications, powered by advanced AI and ML, will revolutionize CRE. AI-driven reliability will become a game changer, with predictive analytics and anomaly detection enabling proactive incident management. CRE teams will harness LLM applications to analyze vast amounts of data, identify patterns, and optimize resource allocation for improved performance and cost-effectiveness. Cultural and organizational transformation will be essential to integrate AI into CRE practices, empowering teams with data-driven decision-making capabilities and AI-augmented problem-solving.

- **Cultural and organizational transformation:** The future of CRE hinges on cultural and organizational transformation. To fully embrace the emerging trends and reap the benefits they offer, organizations must foster a culture of continuous learning, experimentation, and collaboration. Cross-functional teams will become the norm, promoting synergy among development, operations, security, and customer support. A customer-first mindset will drive product development and incident response, ensuring that customer satisfaction remains at the heart of CRE practices. Furthermore, organizations must invest in upskilling their workforce to navigate the complexities of new technologies and AI-driven solutions. Agile and DevOps methodologies will merge with CRE, accelerating development cycles and promoting adaptability in the face of change. Building psychological safety and encouraging innovation will empower teams to take risks and continuously improve, further solidifying the foundation of CRE within the company.

In summary, the future of Lean CRE is undeniably bright, shaped by serverless computing, edge computing, and LLM applications. AI-driven reliability will redefine incident management, while cultural and organizational transformations will pave the way for resilience, adaptability, and customer centricity. As businesses navigate the evolving digital landscape, embracing these trends and aligning with CRE principles will empower them to deliver exceptional reliability and engineering excellence in the era of the cloud and AI.

Chapter 12

Conclusion

We started this book by sharing the value of cloud reliability engineering (CRE). Throughout the book, we introduced multiple CRE concepts and provided practical ways for you to introduce CRE practices in your organizations. No matter what your role is—CEO, CTO, software engineer, or technical program manager—you have an important role to play in bringing CRE practices into your organization. We hope our book provided a foundation for your CRE strategy and gave you food for thought in coming up with the next steps in implementing CRE practices at your company.

We dove deep into how CRE streamlines processes, ensuring that resources are used efficiently and downtime is minimized. But it's not just about the technical side of things—it's also about fostering a collaborative culture where teams can make decisions quickly and feel empowered to innovate. Real-world examples, such as Netflix embracing CRE to ensure uninterrupted service and superior customer experience and Moderna leveraging AWS services for vaccine development, have shown us the tangible benefits of embracing CRE techniques.

So, what's next for engineers and leaders keen on implementing CRE practices in their organizations? Here's a road map to consider.

1. **Get everyone on board:** Start by rallying application teams and getting everyone on the same page about the importance of CRE and how it benefits both internal teams and customers.
2. **Embrace innovation:** Don't shy away from exploring new technologies such as artificial intelligence (AI) and machine learning (ML). These tools can automate tasks, uncover valuable insights, and enhance decision-making processes.

3. **Monitor and adapt:** Keep a close eye on system performance and be ready to adapt as needed. Having robust monitoring and alerting systems in place ensures that you can address issues before they escalate.

4. **Foster collaboration:** Break down silos between teams and encourage collaboration. When everyone is working toward common goals, the results can be truly transformative.

5. **Continuously improve:** Embrace a culture of continuous improvement. Gather feedback, analyze results, and adjust your CRE practices accordingly.

6. **Measure success:** Set clear metrics to track the effectiveness of your CRE efforts. Whether it's uptime, customer satisfaction, or another key indicator, having measurable goals keeps everyone focused.

By following these steps, organizations can pave the way for a more reliable, resilient, and customer-focused approach to operations. It's a journey that requires dedication and effort, but the rewards—increased efficiency, happier customers, and long-term success—are well worth it.

We would like to conclude this book by stating that CRE is not just a new regular practice; it is a strategic imperative. By prioritizing reliability and utilizing AI to do so, businesses mitigate risks, drive innovation, optimize costs, and deliver exceptional customer experiences with new engineering strategies. Embracing CRE principles is a game changer for companies of all sizes and industries, allowing them to thrive in an increasingly competitive and digital-first world.

Incident Response Checklist Template

Description: This template is designed to assist technical teams in efficiently managing and resolving incidents affecting IT systems and services. It's particularly useful in environments where uptime, reliability, and rapid response to issues are critical, such as cloud-based applications, software as a service (SaaS) platforms, and enterprise-level IT operations. Use this template whenever there is an unexpected disruption, a security breach, or any incident that impacts service availability or user experience. The template helps ensure a methodical approach to incident management, from identifying the issue's scope to executing a recovery plan and conducting a postmortem analysis.

Identify the scope of the incident:

What happened?

- Describe the symptoms, indicators, and observations of the incident.
- Identify any potential triggers, such as recent deployments or configuration changes.
- Determine the scope of the incident, including affected services, components, or geographies.
- Specify the nature of the incident (e.g., systems down, security breach, partial or complete inability to access).

Identify the impact:

How critical is the incident?

- Assess the severity of the incident in terms of service loss, impact on specific functions, and business criticality.
- Estimate the number of affected users, customers, or systems.
- Assign a severity level to the incident based on predefined criteria.

Troubleshoot:

- *Cloud provider status*
  - Check for any reported service disruptions or outages by the cloud provider.
  - Identify any dependencies on other services (cloud provider or third party) and investigate reported issues.
- *Monitoring and logs*
  - Review alerts triggered by monitoring tools (e.g., AWS CloudWatch, Azure Monitor, Google Cloud Monitoring).
  - Analyze key metrics and logs for error messages, patterns, or abnormalities.
  - Check for resource issues (CPU, storage, RAM) on cloud instances.
  - Investigate recent configuration changes and their potential impact.
- *Additional considerations*
  - Explore any other potential root causes that may have been missed initially.

Focus on recovery to minimize customer impact:

- *Recovery plan*
  - Determine the plan for restoring data or services using a failover technique, a rollback for compute, or restoration from backup if necessary or by enabling a feature flag.
- *Incident resolution process*
  - Follow the documented process for resolving this type of incident, as outlined in the playbook.

- If the recovery plan does not reflect a standard playbook, go to the next step and ensure that a recovery playbook for that type of incident is created.

Conduct a root cause analysis:

Conduct a postmortem.

- Invite the incident response team, including relevant stakeholders and the site reliability engineering (SRE) team.
- Review the minute-by-minute plan to identify opportunities.
- Allow the app team that owns the compromised service to dive deeper into logs, monitors, and so forth to determine the actual root cause.
- Write an incident summary or incident plan, also known as Correction of Error (COE), with tasks to ensure that this type of incident will not happen again. See one example template in Appendix C.

Notification and communication:

- Notify the incident response team, including relevant stakeholders and leaders.
- Develop a communication plan to inform customers or internal users about the incident.
- Share the next steps and assign responsibilities for their execution, including roles, contact information, frequency of updates, communication channels, and management/user notifications.

Correction of Error (COE) Document Structure

Description: *This template provides a comprehensive framework for documenting and analyzing incidents to drive improvements in system reliability and resilience. It begins with an incident summary tailored for stakeholders, detailing impact, mitigation, and prevention strategies. The impact section quantifies consequences across various dimensions such as financial or reputational, while the timeline offers a chronological account of events with clarity on any gaps. Metrics are used for assessing and monitoring the incident, and critical questions help explore detection, diagnosis, and prevention. The prevention section focuses on root cause analysis using techniques such as the "five whys" to propose effective countermeasures. Action items specify follow-up tasks with responsible parties and deadlines, ensuring accountability. Finally, related items connect to other COEs or documentation, helping contextualize incidents within broader improvement efforts.*

- **Incident summary**
  - Provide a concise overview of the incident.
  - Include details on impact, mitigation efforts, and prevention plans.
  - Write as if communicating to main stakeholders (e.g., CEO).
  - Utilize tools such as AWS Systems Manager Incident Manager.
- **Impact**
  - Quantify the impact on customers and the business.
  - Describe the customer/business impact, severity, and consequences.

- Consider financial, reputational, and operational impacts.
- Analyze the second-order effects and nonfunctional requirements impacted.

- **Timeline**
  - Document events chronologically from incident onset to resolution.
  - Ensure consistency in time zone representation.
  - Include all relevant events and information.
  - Address any gaps in the timeline with clear explanations.

- **Metrics**
  - Define metrics for impact assessment and monitoring.
  - Ensure that the metrics are present to determine the problem and monitor events.

- **Incident questions**
  - Ask key questions to analyze the incident thoroughly.
  - Focus on detection, diagnosis, mitigation, and prevention aspects.
  - Include questions related to customer impact, system restoration, and problem identification.

- **Prevention**
  - Utilize the "five whys" technique to identify root causes.
  - Identify underlying causes and potential prevention measures.
  - Develop a plan to remediate each root cause.
  - Ensure a blame-free approach focused on finding the "why."

- **Action items**
  - Identify actionable activities to improve prevention, diagnosis, or resolution.
  - Specify the priority, responsible person, and due date for each action item.
  - Ensure that the action items are specific, achievable, and time bound.

- **Related items**
  - Reference other relevant COEs or documentation.
  - Provide context for related incidents or events.
  - Help establish connections between different incidents or improvement efforts.

CRE Change Management Checklist

Description: This checklist provides a structured approach to handling changes in cloud environments, ensuring minimal risk and maximum reliability. It emphasizes the importance of having well-defined policies, a documented approval workflow, and a thorough risk assessment to prepare for potential issues. Proper documentation is essential, detailing the reason for the change, a plan, and contingencies such as rollback procedures. Automated testing and validation are recommended to reduce human error, and scheduling should occur during low-traffic periods to lessen user impact. Once changes are implemented, continuous monitoring assesses their effects on system performance, with proactive communication and training keeping all stakeholders informed. A post-implementation review helps gauge success, while regular audits ensure compliance with regulatory standards. This framework ensures that changes are well planned, effectively executed, and aligned with broader operational and regulatory requirements.

1. **Change management policies:** Deploying new applications, updating software, or modifying configurations requires different policies.
2. **Approval workflow:** Follow all the steps, create records, and provide change history for any change. Each change should go through the CRE approval process.

3. **Risk assessment:** There is risk associated with any change, so it is important to assess risks and set risk mitigation or avoidance, as required.

4. **Change management documentation:** The documentation should include the reason, a plan, and a approval workflow. It is critical that each change request includes a back-out procedure in case of any issues. If required, rollback should be fast and error free. Other contingency planning efforts may be required.

5. **Testing and validation:** While a deep dive into testing and validation requires a separate book, it is important to have tests automated to avoid human error. In addition, there are multiple testing techniques that allow testing in a production-like environment. If this is possible, the latter is preferable.

6. **Scheduling:** The change is scheduled at a specific time that is announced in advance, and it is usually implemented during quiet hours. For example, banking applications are updated during outside-of-trading hours or during holiday closures.

7. **Monitoring and alerting:** Once the change is completed, monitoring and alerting are continuously assessing the impact of the change on system reliability and performance. This data informs the success or failure of the performed change.

8. **Communication and training:** Communication and training are extremely important. First, the change needs to be communicated to all impacted stakeholders. Second, all relevant groups need to be aware of the change and receive corresponding training, if required, based on their function. For example, service center representatives need communication (and sometimes training) for new features deployed to production that are available to the customer.

9. **Post-implementation review:** Once the change is communicated, a post-implementation review is usually scheduled after a specific time to collect sufficient metrics to determine if the change was successful.

10. **Audit and compliance:** Once the change is approved, it becomes part of the upcoming compliance and audit to ensure that the system complies with all government and industry regulations and standards for a specific geography and business.

Glossary

Agile—An iterative approach to software development that prioritizes customer collaboration, adaptability, and early delivery.

Artificial intelligence (AI)—The simulation of human intelligence in machines, which allows them to perform tasks that typically require human intelligence.

Blameless culture—An organizational culture that focuses on learning from failures and mistakes rather than blaming individuals.

Chaos engineering—The practice of intentionally introducing controlled and well-monitored chaos or failures into a system to test its resilience and identify potential weaknesses.

CI/CD—Continuous integration and continuous delivery are practices that automate the process of integrating code changes and deploying software.

Cloud engineering—The practice of designing, developing, and maintaining cloud-based systems and services to ensure reliability and efficiency.

Cloud provider—An organization that offers cloud computing services, providing infrastructure, platforms, and software over the internet to users.

Cloud reliability engineering (CRE)—The practice of ensuring the dependability and availability of cloud-based services and systems to meet user expectations.

Continuous improvement—An ongoing effort to enhance products, services, and processes by making incremental changes based on feedback and data.

Correction of Error (COE)—Amazon's standard mechanism for post-incident analysis. This lets us analyze a system after an incident to avoid recurrences in the future. These incidents also help us learn more about how our systems and processes work. That knowledge often leads to actions that help other incident scenarios, not just the prevention of a specific recurrence.

DevOps—A collaborative approach that integrates development and operations teams to improve software delivery and reliability.

Domain name system (DNS)—A fundamental component of the internet that serves as a distributed naming system used to map human-friendly domain names to IP (Internet Protocol) addresses. Domain names are the familiar web addresses (e.g., www.google.com) that people use to access websites and online services. These names are easier for humans to remember than numerical IP addresses.

Error budget—The acceptable level of system unreliability, used in site reliability engineering (SRE) to balance new feature development and system stability.

"Five whys" analysis—Lean problem-solving technique used to identify the root cause of an issue by repeatedly asking "why" to explore deeper causes.

Game days—Game days, from a cloud reliability engineering (CRE) perspective, refer to structured and planned exercises conducted by engineering teams to simulate and test how a cloud-based system responds to various failure scenarios and stress conditions.

Generative AI models—These models can generate new data similar to the data they were trained on. In the context of CRE, generative AI (GenAI) can be used to simulate potential failure scenarios, creating synthetic data for testing and validation of systems under various conditions.

Kaizen—A Japanese term for "continuous improvement," involving small, frequent changes to improve efficiency and quality.

Kanban—A visual management system used to control and optimize work processes, promoting efficiency and reducing waste.

Large language models (LLMs)—Deep learning models that can understand and generate humanlike text based on the data they were trained on. LLMs can be used in CRE for tasks such as automated incident response, documentation generation, and real-time troubleshooting guidance.

Lean—A methodology focused on minimizing waste and maximizing value in processes, emphasizing continuous improvement and flow.

Lean CRE—The application of Lean principles to the design, development, and maintenance of cloud-based systems, focusing on reliability.

Machine learning (ML)—A subset of AI, ML involves training algorithms on large datasets to identify patterns and make predictions. For CRE, ML can be invaluable in predictive maintenance, anomaly detection, and capacity planning.

Mean time to detect (MTTD)—The average time it takes to detect an incident or problem within a system, which is used to improve incident response times.

Mean time to recover (MTTR)—The average time it takes to restore a system or service to normal operation after an incident or failure.

Metrics—Quantifiable measurements used to assess and track the performance, quality, and efficiency of cloud systems and engineering processes.

Minimum lovable product (MLP)—A minimal version of a product, with just enough features to gather feedback and validate assumptions before full development while ensuring that it provides customer value and delights its customers.

Objectives and key results (OKRs)—A goal-setting framework that defines objectives and the measurable outcomes that indicate progress and achievement of those objectives.

Operational excellence—The practice of efficiently and effectively managing cloud resources and services to ensure the reliability, availability, and performance of applications and systems hosted in the cloud.

Reliability—The ability of a system to perform its intended function consistently and predictably, meeting user needs without failure or downtime.

Resilience—The ability of a system to withstand and recover from failures, ensuring continuous operation and minimal impact on users.

Scalability—The capability of a system to handle increased workload and growth, adapting to changing demands without sacrificing performance.

Scrum—An Agile framework for managing and organizing work, involving short, fixed-length iterations called sprints.

Serverless engineering—A cloud computing model in which cloud providers manage the infrastructure, allowing developers to focus on building application logic.

Service level agreement (SLA)—A formal agreement that outlines the expected level of service reliability and consequences for not meeting the service level objectives (SLOs).

Service level objective (SLO)—A target for the reliability of a service, used to measure its performance and ensure that it meets user expectations.

Site reliability engineering (SRE)—A discipline that combines software engineering and operations to build and maintain reliable, scalable cloud systems.

Time to detect (TTD)—A critical metric in the field of incident management and cloud reliability engineering. It represents the amount of time it takes to identify and become aware of an incident or issue within a system or application from the moment it first occurs. TTD measures the speed and efficiency with which an organization can detect anomalies, deviations, or problems that might impact the performance, availability, or security of its digital services.

Time to recover (TTR)—A crucial metric in the context of incident management and cloud reliability engineering. It represents the amount of time required to fully restore a system, service, or application to its normal operational state after an incident or disruption has occurred. TTR measures the speed and efficiency with which an organization can recover from an incident, minimizing downtime and the associated impact on users and business operations.

User story—A concise description of a feature from an end user's perspective, used in Agile to communicate requirements and value.

Value stream mapping—A Lean technique used to analyze and optimize the steps and flow of processes, identifying areas for improvement.

Virtual private cloud (VPS)—A fundamental building block in cloud computing, allowing organizations to create and manage their network infrastructure in the cloud. VPC provides the flexibility to design complex network topologies while maintaining security and isolation between different environments and workloads.

References

Chapter 1

Page 5: Dr. Werner Vogels, quoted in "Forming a Chaos Engineering Team." AWS. https://maturitymodel.security.aws.dev/en/4.-optimized/chaos-engineering/

Page 5: Mark Russinovich. "With Performance Testing in Azure." Microsoft Azure Blog. https://azure.microsoft.com/en-us/blog/advancing-application-reliability-with-performance-testing-in-azure/

Page 18: Liam Tung. "Google details 'catastrophic' cloud outage events: Promises to do better next time." 1Password. June 7, 2019. https://www.zdnet.com/article/google-details-catastrophic-cloud-outage-events-promises-to-do-better-next-time/

Page 18: Richard Speed. "Microsoft Azure: It's getting hot in here, so shut down all your cores." The Register. September 4, 2018. https://www.theregister.com/2018/09/04/azure_its_getting_hot_in_here/

Page 19: Darrell Etherington. "Amazon AWS S3 outage is breaking things for a lot of websites and apps." TechCrunch. February 28, 2017. https://techcrunch.com/2017/02/28/amazon-aws-s3-outage-is-breaking-things-for-a-lot-of-websites-and-apps/

Page 19: Russell, Jon. The world's largest DDoS attack took GitHub offline for fewer than 10 minutes, on March 2, 2018. https://techcrunch.com/2018/03/02/the-worlds-largest-ddos-attack-took-github-offline-for-less-than-tens-minutes/

Page 19: Cloudinary. "Chaos Engineering: Finding Failures Before They Become Outages." January 14, 2020. https://res.cloudinary.com/gremlin/image/upload/v1579028841/20200114_Chaos_Engineering_White_Paper.pdf

Page 20: Laura DiDio. "The Cost of Enterprise Downtime." TechChannel. September 30, 2021. https://techchannel.com/IT-Strategy/09/2021/cost-enterprise-downtime

Page 20: Laura DiDio. "Hourly Cost of Downtime." Laura's Insights ITIC Blog, Information Technology Intelligence Consulting. https://itic-corp.com/tag/hourly-cost-of-downtime/#:~:text=ITIC's%202021%20Hourly%20Cost%20of,(SMEs)%20and%20large%20enterprises

Chapter 2

Page 36: "Resiliency Checklist for Specific Azure Services." Microsoft Azure Architecture Center, July 26, 2023. https://learn.microsoft.com/en-us/azure/architecture/checklist/resiliency-per-service

Page 36: "Patterns for Scalable and Resilient Apps." Google Cloud Architecture Center. Last reviewed March 19, 2024. https://cloud.google.com/architecture/scalable-and-resilient-apps

Page 43: "AZ Availability: Power Interruption." Amazon Web Services. https://docs.aws.amazon.com/fis/latest/userguide/az-availability-scenario.html

Chapter 3

Page 56: "Replicate Data Within and Between AWS Regions Using Amazon S3 Replication." Amazon Web Services. https://aws.amazon.com/getting-started/hands-on/replicate-data-using-amazon-s3-replication/

Page 56: "Amazon RDS Multi-AZ." Amazon Web Services. https://aws.amazon.com/rds/features/multi-az/

Page 57: "Object Storage for Companies of All Sizes." Google Cloud Storage. https://cloud.google.com/storage

Page 57: "Always On Database with Virtually Unlimited Scale." Google Cloud Spanner. https://cloud.google.com/spanner

Page 57: "Azure Backup." Microsoft Azure Cloud Backup. https://azure.microsoft.com/en-us/products/backup

Page 57: "Active Geo-Replication." Microsoft Learn Challenge. September 27, 2024. https://learn.microsoft.com/en-us/azure/azure-sql/database/active-geo-replication-overview?view=azuresql

Chapter 4

Page 79: Atlassian. *Incident Management Handbook for Jira Service Management.* https://www.atlassian.com/incident-management/handbook/postmortems

Page 80: Luis Caro, Jose Luis Caro, Juan Ossa, and Johnny Hanley. "Why Should You Develop a Correction of Error (COE)." Amazon Web Services. February 18, 2022. https://aws.amazon.com/blogs/mt/why-you-should-develop-a-correction-of-error-coe/

Page 82: Juan Ossa and Johnny Hanley. "Creating a Correction of Errors Document." AWS Cloud Operations Blog, November 6, 2023. https://aws.amazon.com/blogs/mt/creating-a-correction-of-errors-document/

Page 89: AWS Well-Architected Framework, Correction of Error. Amazon Web Services. https://wa.aws.amazon.com/wat.concept.coe.en.html

Page 82: John Lunney and Sue Lueder. Postmortem culture: Learning from failure. In: Niall Richard Murphy, Betsy Beyer, Chris Jones, Jennifer Petoff (Eds.), *Site Reliability Engineering* (O'Reilly Media, 2016).

Chapter 5

Page 106: "AT&T Improves Operations and Employee Experiences with Azure and AI Technologies." Microsoft Customer Stories. May 18, 2023. https://www.microsoft.com/en/customers/story/1637511309136244127-att-telecommunications-azure-openai-service

Page 106: Wikipedia definition of generative AI. https://en.wikipedia.org/wiki/Generative_artificial_intelligence

Chapter 6

Page 112: Taiichi Ohno. *Toyota Production System: Beyond Large-Scale Production* (Productivity Press, 1988).

Page 114: Mary Poppendieck and Tom Poppendieck. *Lean Software Development: An Agile Toolkit* (Addison-Wesley, 2003).

Chapter 10

Page 191: Google's definition of "psychological safety." https://www.thinkwithgoogle.com/intl/en-emea/consumer-insights/consumer-trends/five-dynamics-effective-team

Chapter 11

Page 206: Forbes: Rafael Umann. "To Take Software Development to the Next Level, Consider the Benefits of Serverless Computing." Forbes, May 2023. https://www.forbes.com/sites/forbestechcouncil/2023/05/17/to-take-software-development-to-the-next-level-consider-the-benefits-of-serverless-computing/?sh=2f5741541b9c

Page 206: Deloitte. "Understand the Market: The 5G and Edge Computing Revolution. Tapping into the Power of 5G and Edge Computing Opportunities." July 2023. https://www2.deloitte.com/us/en/pages/consulting/solutions/tapping-into-the-power-of-5g-and-edge-computing-opportunities.html

Page 207: McKinsey Digital. "Driving Impact at Scale from Automation and AI." February 2019. https://www.mckinsey.com/capabilities/mckinsey-digital/our-insights/driving-impact-at-scale-from-automation-and-ai

Page 209: Nordstrom case study, "How Nordstrom Transformed Its Infrastructure Using a Serverless Architecture." 2021. https://aws.amazon.com/solutions/case-studies/nordstrom/

Page 209: Moderna case study. "Moderna on AWS." 2022. https://aws.amazon.com/solutions/case-studies/innovators/moderna/

Index